MW01244888

ROCK YOUR CITY

5 Steps to Becoming The Biggest Band in Town

BY JOHN MICHALAK
WITH DAN CULL

ROCK YOUR CITY:
5 STEPS TO BECOMING THE BIGGEST BAND IN TOWN
Copyright © 2012 by GORILLA PUBLISHING

ISBN (978-0-9854125-1-7)

Edited by Anthony Powers
Assistant Editors: Dan Bliss, Natalie Cull, & Bryan Pauley
Book Coach: Bobbi Linkemer
Cover Design by Doan Buu
Interior Layout by Anthony Powers
Conceptual Assistance: Alessa Michalak, Anthony Powers, & Ashley Grey

GORILLA PUBLISHING

DEDICATION

I dedicate this book to my wife, Heather, and my daughter, Alessa, for their love and support—the two people in the world that know how to make me laugh the hardest. I love you both so much.

TABLE OF CONTENTS

Acknowledgments
Contents
Introduction

Step 1: Use Your Social Circle to Create a Massive Fan Base

Step 2: Create and Put On Outstanding Shows

Step 3: Write Great Songs

Step 4: Make Genuine Connections with Your Fans

Step 5: Create Name Recognition

ACKNOWLEDGEMENTS

I would like to thank everyone that that helped with this book, starting with my beautiful wife Heather.

Heather - Thank you for being so understanding through-out this process. I never dreamed that I would find a wife as loving and understanding as you have been. How you put up with my 101 projects a week work ethic, I will never know.

Alessa - Thank you for all your help with the book, and for being honest with me when my writing was a little too pompous. I am really glad that I always told you the truth while you were growing up, it really paid off. You're a wonderful daughter; I am blessed to have you in my life.

Dan - Thank you for all your help, not just as a co-author, but also, as an amazing business partner, brother and friend. You're the most optimistic person I know, and you're my rock when things are falling apart.

Anthony - Thank you so much for all your help with the book. There is no way that this book that I am so proud of would be half of what it is without all of your help. I will be *eternally* grateful.

Natalie - Thank you for your help with the book. I know you have your hands full at home with three wonderful children. For you to make the time to help, means the world to me.

Bobbi - Thank you for help, I learned so much from you. I am really glad that when I went looking for a book coach, I found you. The difference in my writing from the day I hired you is tenfold.

Bryan - Thank you for your help, I also learned a lot from you. I feel like You, Bobbi, and Anthony, have given me a college education regarding the English language.

The Gorilla Staff, Past and Present - Thank you so much. Your efforts day in and day out have helped to develop the strategies presented in this book. Without your hard work, this book would never have been possible, and for that I am grateful.

My Loving Family and Friends - All my life, I have been considered the dreamer, first with my rock n roll, then with my business ventures, now with my writing. I thank all of you for your love and support, and I truly hope that you all know how much I love you.

Mom, thanks for always being there for me. Dad, thank you for believing in me when I needed your help, you'll never know how much your help has changed my life. Gary, you've been wonderful to all of us, thank you so much. Gigi, thanks for treating me like a son, thanks for treating all my brothers and sisters like they were your own, we all love you. Kelly, thanks for being so strong, I am the older brother, you're supposed to look up to me, instead I am always finding myself looking up to you. Kim, thanks for being so loving, you must be the nicest person on the planet. Aidan thanks for being in my life. I have always and will always think of as my son. You're a great kid and I am very proud of you. Adriana and Alex, thanks for being the cutest two grandchildren ever. John thanks for being so wonderful to my daughter. Joe, thanks for being there when I needed you, you're not just my best friend, but everyone's best friend. Dan Bliss, thanks for everything, you are my friend, and my brother.

CONTENTS

INTRODUCTION

I have been planning to write a book on the music business for over ten years now. In fact, I wrote a sample chapter back in 2002 and we even hired a book agent who got us a deal with a small publisher. Unfortunately, the deal didn't make sense to us at the time, so we passed. In retrospect, maybe we should have taken it. No, it wasn't the greatest deal ever, but I would have been motivated to finish the book years ago, and I would probably be on my fourth of fifth book by now, instead of just finishing up my first. In life, the value one gets from experience is priceless, and my decision to pass on the old deal cost me some of that life experience—or at least delayed it.

Even though I first decided to write a book on the music business only ten years ago, in some ways, I have been preparing for it all my life. My parents bought me my first guitar when I was fourteen years old. It was supposed to be a Christmas present, but for some reason they gave it to me in August.

I had decided I wanted to be in a band after my friends crowned me king of the air-guitar; we would get goofy and play air-guitar to our favorite Kiss songs. I'm surprised we weren't walking around in Kiss make-up since that's all we talked about. We had every one of their albums, tons of magazines with articles about them, and our rooms were covered in Kiss posters.

A year later, we all had instruments and we formed our first band together. I took on the role of band manager and spent more time planning our practices and looking for opportunities to perform than I can remember. Our first real big show was a talent show, although it was more like a battle of the bands, since half the acts were bands. We signed up for this show after a solid year of practicing in my parent's basement, which we soundproofed with neon pink and yellow shag carpeting and hundreds of crusty old egg cartons. Puberty changed that basement from our suburban tree house to our band practice space.

At this show, we won three awards, more than any other group. Ironically, the only other musical group to win an award that night was a lip syncing, air-guitar playing band fronted by none other than Mike Shea, the owner of AP Magazine. If I remember correctly, they covered a Judas Priest song.

Mike's group went on to take first place in the talent show that night. We all had a great time. I might have only been about 15 years old, but that night is still one of the top-ten greatest moments in my life. To see and hear the crowd roar made me feel like I was on top of the world. In a lot of ways, I owe music everything. It is my hope that this book can give a little back.

5 STEPS TO BECOMING THE BIGGEST BAND IN TOWN:

1. **SONGS**
2. **OUTSTANDING LIVE SHOWS**
3. **NAME RECOGNITION**
4. **GENUINE FANS**
5. **SOCIAL CIRCLE**

STEP 1:
Use Your
SOCIAL CIRCLE
to Create a
Massive Fan Base

Does Your Group Exist?

"I don't exist when you don't see me."

- Sisters of Mercy

You're Invisible

When I first started playing in a live band, I would hang flyers and promote our shows vigorously. I believed people would come out in droves because we were an exceptional band. At that time, this reasoning seemed logical to me. Why not? All the other local bands were promoting their shows with flyers or by getting the clubs to add their name to the club's print ads. Unfortunately, I had to learn the hard way that there is no correlation between how good a local group may be and how many people come to see them.

Back then, if all the bands on a particular show (concert) were good, or we were playing in an awesome club, I would automatically assume the place would be packed. I can't begin to tell you how many times I was disappointed when we played to a relatively empty room. Nevertheless, every time we booked a show, I posted flyers around town and told myself that *this* time, things would be different; *this* show was going to be crowded. Why? Well, *this* time, we were playing at a better club, on a better night, or there was some other factor that made me believe that *this time* we would attract a big crowd.

I didn't know it then, but I was putting my energy in the wrong place. I was working hard to promote something that was not promotable. Here is what I mean: it is not possible to generate interest in a band that no one has ever heard of simply by hanging up flyers, around town. Yes, it was cool to see our group's name in print; but no one knew our group or our music outside our circle of friends. And even *some of them* had never really *listened* to our music. Yet, I kept repeating the same pattern, each time expecting different results. First, I posted 100 flyers, and no one came. Next, I posted 300 flyers, and no one came. Finally, I posted 1,000 flyers but got the same result: no one came.

TIP: When playing in a concert club, a concert hall, or a theater, bring a crowd. These types of venues do not have built-in audiences.

I didn't understand that it didn't matter how good we were, since we were unknown. Our group didn't exist outside our own circle of friends, family, or coworkers. We weren't getting any airplay; we didn't even have a record yet. The rest of the world had no idea who we were, what we looked like, how we sounded, or anything else about us. Sad to say, we were invisible. And we weren't unusual. Most local groups had never released a record or had their music played on the radio. Most local groups are as invisible as we were.

Here is what I learned: people do not magically turn out for a group they have never heard of. Concert clubs, concert halls, and theaters do not have built-in audiences. People don't just show up at a club and ask, "Who's playing tonight?" This may be the most misunderstood concept in the concert business. What I didn't realize then is so obvious to me now. If no one outside your circle of friends and family has ever heard your music, then no one outside that circle is going to come to your next concert.

I completely missed that point. The question is, are you missing it as well? If so, it is time to stop repeating strategies that don't work and learn some that will. In this chapter, I will explain why promotion—as most of us understand that word—is an ineffective way to build your fan base. I will show you exactly what to do instead.

Promotion Will Fail

Promotion usually takes the form of a publicity campaign for a particular product, organization, or venture. In our business, most local groups think they need to promote themselves or hire someone to do it for them. The strategies they seem to favor include posting flyers or getting their group's name in print, on the radio, or featured in a news story.

What I have learned from working with thousands of groups is that none of these activities do anything to affect attendance at a local show, or to grow a local band. Not even radio helps, unless the station actually *plays* a local group's music. Stations rarely do this, unless it's for a local radio show that features local music. Even then, it's often very late at night with a very small listening audience. (Radio stations usually charges hundreds of dollars for a one-minute ad during the day; that same ad running on a Sunday night might cost as little as $5. That ad cost should give you an idea of the size of the audiences for late-night shows.) In instances where a station does play a local group's music, it's usually only once, which is not enough for anyone to know if they like a song.

My business partner and co-author, Dan Cull, and I own a concert production company called Gorilla Music. We coordinate an average of twenty local shows a week, with about ten groups on each show, in more than sixty-five U.S. markets. After coordinating shows with thousands of bands across the country, I have never seen a local group successfully reach the top of its market on promotion alone.

While traditional promotion may be effective for tangible products, there is a big difference between promoting a tangible product and an intangible one. Music is intangible. That makes music one of the most difficult products to explain and the reason why most groups have so much trouble describing their own sound. Even if a group can pinpoint their genre or make comparisons to other artists, it's still not the same as having someone listen to their music. People won't know if they're going to like a group's music until they've heard it for themselves. When was the last time you walked into a record store and bought a bunch of CDs or gone to a show to see a group you've never heard of?

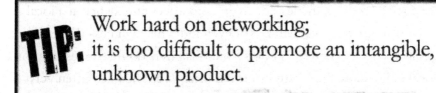

TIP: Work hard on networking; it is too difficult to promote an intangible, unknown product.

Therein rests the biggest problem for the aspiring artist: it is very difficult to get your music on commercial radio where thousands of people will hear it; yet, that is a critical component of attracting pcople to your shows. For people to become fans of your music, they have to experience it first-hand... multiple times.

Social Media?

Yes, social media and video sharing sites are extremely useful tools for sharing your music. However, these tools have not made a measurable impact on a vast majority of local artist's record sales or tickets sales for their shows. For the last few years, unidentified artists have bombarded Internet users with local music. Unfortunately, most of the music hasn't been very good, and this has turned off millions of potential fans.

So, if you can't rely on social media sites to spread the word, what is the alternative? The answer is simple: you have to get out there in the trenches and literally drag people to your shows. You must do this until your concerts are so packed that you've established a reputation for having great shows.

This does not mean you should abandon your Facebook or YouTube accounts. Social networking sites like ReverbNation are a great way to reach your current fans, and some people may take a chance and give your music a listen. If enough people tell each other about your great songs or sound, and you really catch on, that's called "going viral." (It's also called a miracle.) It's not likely, but miracles have been known to happen. So, stay on top of all your social networking sites and use them to complement your word-of-mouth marketing activities. Used properly social networking sites are the best tools local bands have available to them. Word of mouth marketing in conjunction with social networking is how you will make the biggest impact on selling your music and packing your shows.

The Reason Fans Come

Two things to keep in mind: 1) At the local level, clubs and promoters are event coordinators, not promoters, even if they tell you they can promote your band; 2) The quality of your music at this stage of your career has very little to do with the number of people who will come to see you.

How many times have you seen good or even great groups play in front of no one? It happens all the time. Have you seen a terrible group play at a packed venue? That happens often as well. How can less talented groups draw bigger crowds than more talented groups? The answer has to do with whether people are enjoying themselves.

That's not to say that the quality of the music isn't important. It is. However, the music is not the driving motivation for people attending a local show. I know; this is a concert, and people go to concerts for the music, right? Well, yes and no. On one hand, they go for the music; but it has to be music they've heard before, music they like.

The local band has a different challenge than the famous touring acts. Remember the chicken or the egg riddle? For the touring act, the music comes first. You like their music, so you go and see them in concert. It rarely happens this way for local groups. When you go to see a friend's band perform live, this is often the first time you have heard their music.

If people don't go to local shows for the music, then why do they go? Mostly, they go to have fun and to hang out with friends and like-minded people. They go because someone invited them, or to be a part of a scene, or to meet new people, or to see their secret crush. There are many reasons, but hearing unfamiliar music usually isn't the main one.

When you get in your car and drive to the local arena or music hall to see your favorite national act, chances are you listen to that group's music on the way to the concert. You listen or jam to the songs you're about to hear in a live setting. If you're in a local group and people are singing along to your songs in their cars, you're on your way to developing true fans. I will talk more about true fans in the chapter, "Selling Your Music." Right now, you need to understand that people go to shows to have fun, and they have more fun if there is a crowd. People like to go where they can be with other people who are sharing their experience. If you are able to pack a venue full of people, your fans will have more fun and be much more likely to come for your next show.

 Get your fans to sing along to one of your songs. This will make your event more memorable and more fun for them.

Create a Network; Create a Buzz

If promotion is largely ineffective for local talent, what's the alternative? The answer is *networking*—meeting new people, making new connections, and recruiting people to attend your shows. This is the most effective way to grow your fan base, as you will see in the next two chapters.

Networking is powerful. Networking is the best way to create buzz around your group. Networking is easy, natural, and free. The more people you know, the better. Every one of these people knows other people—lots of other people. Networking is all about meeting as many of those people as you can and getting the those people to attend

JUST ONE PACKED SHOW. Once they attend a sold-out show, the buzz will follow. It may be impossible to describe your sound, but it's not hard to say, "These guys are great. I love their music, and their show was so much fun! It was packed to the walls!" Pretty soon, the word is out, faster than you would have ever believed.

TIP: Try to get photos of your band in front of huge crowds. By posting these photos on your ReverbNation page you will attract more people to your next show.

The more people you can get out to your shows, the more fun your friends will have, and the more likely it is that they will come again. If they have a great time, they will also tell others about your group. People who spread the word are exactly what you need; it's the most effective way to grow your fan base. This is the way to create a buzz around your band. Once you create that buzz, great things will start to happen. Can you imagine what the local music scene across this country would be like if every group could bring at least 100 people to every show? Frankly, that's my dream—to build every local scene in every city in this country. I sincerely hope that you will join me in realizing this dream, and while you may have your doubts right now, I assure you it is well within your power to do so.

RECAP

- There is no correlation between the quality of your music and the size of your crowds if no one has heard your music before.

- Unknown groups don't exist outside their own circle of friends, family, or coworkers.

- People do not magically turn out for a group they have never heard of. Concert clubs, concert halls, and theaters do not have built-in audiences

- There is a big difference between promoting a tangible product and an intangible one. Music is intangible.

- Old-fashioned promotions are an ineffective way to grow a local group's fan base.

- The most powerful way to get people to your shows is by networking. Networking is free, easy, and highly-effective for local groups.

CHAPTER 2

Exposure Doesn't Work

"Giving a good performance, giving it all is what it's all about.

I love to perform."

- Henry Rollins

Why Play Live?

I have been interviewing and consulting with groups for years. During that time, I have asked hundreds of groups why they play live. I get some pretty strange looks, usually followed by an awkward pause while they try to make sense of my question. Then they respond with something like "because we love it" or "it's our passion." I don't leave it there; I ask again, "What are some of the other reasons you play live?" The next most popular answer is "for exposure." They don't always call it exposure, but that's essentially, what they're talking about. The other two popular answers are "to make money" and to "gain more experience playing live." The irony is that only two of these answers will further their careers; the rest could actually hinder them more than they realize.

The first and most popular answer—"because we love it"—is definitely the reason most groups perform live. It may be your reason, too. It's very difficult to explain that the very thing you love, the reason you play music, could prevent you from advancing your career. Your love for performing should *never* be a factor in deciding which show opportunities to accept or how often to play live locally. Unfortunately, it usually ends up being the only factor groups use to make these decisions. You love playing live so much that you take every gig you can get from anyone who will offer you a show. Unfortunately, playing lots of gigs will *not* help your group develop a strong local draw. Your group needs a strong draw, so you can get good gigs and show opportunities, sometimes life-changing opportunities.

The other favorite answer, "exposure," is also not a good reason to perform live. In fact, local exposure doesn't help a group's draw either, which I will explain in detail throughout this chapter. *The best reasons to perform live are to gain experience, to make money or raise capital, and to network,* all of which are necessary if you want to make it to the next level. If you're in a group that hopes one day to write, record, and perform music for a living, you need more experience, capital, and a bigger network to help you move up the ladder.

We Worshiped Exposure

I was in two groups in my early twenties. The first was a band called Serious Nature. I met a few guys at a local recording studio, and they gave me an opportunity to audition for their group. They were looking for a bass player, and at the time, that's exactly what I played—bass. Tim, the drummer, was an upbeat salesman type, and funny as hell. The guitarist, Ted, was super friendly and a little quirky. The lead singer and keyboard player, Mike, was a talented musician and hard-working entrepreneur. Tim and Mike were both in their late twenties and had lots of experience. They were great people; I looked up to both of them and felt blessed to have been given the opportunity to play with them.

I joined their group and learned all the songs. Within a very short time, we were playing live. At our very first show, we had more than fifty people there, just to see us. A week later, we had our second show, and only about thirty people showed up. We kept playing as many shows as we could get, any place that would have us. Within a few months, we couldn't get anyone out to our shows, and I mean no one! There were times when we couldn't even get our girlfriends out to see us. We kept on playing show after show, sometimes three or four shows a week. I remember playing a show on a Saturday afternoon and then another one that night. These were sandwiched between a show on Friday night and another one Sunday night. We most likely played over 100 shows in the first year I was with them.

From time to time, we would get to play for a decent crowd, but it was always the headliner's crowd, not ours. And we knew it. Every time we would venture out and land a headlining show of our own, we wouldn't get more than a handful of people, and the venue would be empty. We kept saying we needed more exposure and more shows. We thought we needed more people to see us. It seemed to make sense. We were a talented group, and the people who did catch our set would tell us how much they loved us.

Then, two things happened. The first was an amazing opportunity to open for a hot, new act called Exposé that was touring the country after having a big hit on radio called "Seasons Change." We opened the show to a sold-out crowd of about 2,000 people, mostly screaming girls. After the show, I felt like a rock star with girls everywhere asking for autographs and flirting with us. I remember thinking that this was the opportunity we needed, that this gig was going to change everything. I assumed that all these screaming girls would be at our next show, but they weren't. I never saw any of them again.

The second thing that happened was incredible. We had just recorded our first record and released a single called "Rescue Me." Tim, our drummer and band manager, was able to convince the local Top 40 station in town to play it. When they played it for the first time, I almost cried. I thought I had made it. I had dreams of MTV, touring, hit singles, and fame. At that time, Tim was a schoolteacher for a junior high school. After the station played our song, he had all his students call the station and request it over and over (for extra credit of course!). Most of his students and the rest of the school got behind him and blew up the request lines. Our song went into rotation and got all the way up to number eight. I would hear it playing all day long. Again, I had visions of stardom, and I couldn't wait for our next headlining show.

We were riding high on the success of our new single, and we booked our next headlining show at a club called The Phantasy. We found a few opening acts, made flyers, and distributed them everywhere. Then, we showed up for our show, but no one else did. We had fewer than thirty people there to see us. We were shocked.

The students who had been requesting our song were too young to get in, and no one else had any interest in our supposed "hit" song. I was devastated and confused. How could we have a song on the radio and still not have any fans? It was quite baffling. Years later, after buying my own concert club and promoting concerts for many national touring acts; I finally understood what had happened. If I hadn't become a club owner, I would never have learned the truth.

The Songs Must Be Good

In 1995, I bought my first club—a popular concert club called Peabody's. Everyone from Pearl Jam and Green Day to Tori Amos and Jane's Addiction had played there before. As my business partner and I took over, we started learning the business and trying to build relationships. It was a tough business, but also a great life experience for me.

Early on, I realized that some of the "baby national acts" would sell out our club, and some couldn't get anyone out to see them. A baby national act is a group that is just starting out, a group that may have one song on the radio and a record label to support it. For example, the first time Creed played my club, no one came. Radio was playing the hell out of their record, but fewer than fifty people were at their show. The same thing was true for Tonic. Tonic played at my club three times that first year with the same result. Finally, as you may know, both Creed and Tonic had big songs that took off. That's when their careers took off as well.

It was around this time that I began to understand why no one had come to see our group, even though we had a song on the radio. I learned that if a song on the radio touches people, they come out in droves to see that group. If it doesn't touch people, they won't bother. Just having a song on the radio means nothing; it has to *affect* people to get them off their couches and into the club. Our song just didn't touch anyone. Even though the request line was ringing off the hook, it was fabricated interest. Don't get me wrong. If our song had truly moved people, all those phone calls would have helped to catapult that song and our group to the top. However, that wasn't the case.

 TIP: Write songs that have the ability to move people. People are less likely to see a new band, unless their songs affect them in some way.

I didn't know any of this back then. We had a talented group that was getting lots of exposure, opening for national acts, getting airtime on the radio, and playing show after show. Yet, we couldn't fill up a small living room with our draw. What were we doing wrong? Everything!

The Invention of Pre-Sale Tickets

When I left Serious Nature, I met Richard Patrick, formerly of Nine Inch Nails (NIN) and front man for Filter. He was a charismatic singer and guitarist from Bay Village, Ohio. When I met Richard he was in a group called The Act, and had just lost his bass player. We started working together and re-formed his group. We kept the drummer, a young kid named Dave, who was also from Bay Village. We added a local keyboard player named Frank who had lots of experience and talent. Frank had played with a few very successful local groups—one called the Exotic Birds with Trent Reznor of NIN and Andy Kubiszewski of Stabbing Westward and The The. After we re-formed the band, we renamed it The AKT, which was Richard's idea. I loved the new name.

The first thing we did was write and record for a full year. Richard and I worked almost every night on our music and our plan for success. Then, we booked our first show, and we gave ourselves four months to promote it (I use the term *promote* very loosely). Ironically, we booked our first show at the club I would buy seven years later, Peabody's, the most prominent concert club in town. We asked the club owner at the time—Tony Ciulla (who later went on to manage Marilyn Manson)—for 200 pre-sale tickets. It was the first time anyone in town had even heard of pre-sale tickets for a local group. Apparently, the practice was popular in Los Angeles, but I had never heard of it. Frankly, I thought I had invented the concept of pre-sale tickets.

Now, we didn't get tickets with the notion that we were promoting our show. Our goal was to raise working capital for recording, and to help us release a record. So, we got 200 pre-sale tickets from the club in order to raise money, which is what we did. We sold all 200 tickets and raised $1,000 dollars.

We also took a portion of the money we made from ticket sales and bought T-shirts. We sold most of the shirts before our very first show. Then, we made posters and flyers to paper the town. Richard and I went out almost every night after practice to drink beer and promote our show. Well, we thought we were promoting, but really, we were *networking*. We went out so often that, after a little while; we would run into the same people repeatedly. We would always remind them about our show and we would try to sell tickets or a T-shirt on the spot.

We used the rest of the money we made from ticket and T-shirt sales and started recording. We bought some equipment, then rented and borrowed the rest of what we needed. After we recorded a few songs, we released a single in a cassette format to college radio. Back then, college DJs would play cassette tapes, records, anything they could get their hands on. We gave a cassette single to every college station in town, set up a few college radio interviews, and made sure that every college jock who played music in our genre had one of our tapes. Immediately, local college radio picked up on one of our songs, and I would hear it on different stations all day long.

Next, we created a huge industry guest list. We invited more than 500 people who worked in the industry to our show, as well as every college and commercial DJ from every station in town. We invited every person who liked alternative rock and worked at a local recording studio, music store, or concert club. We went to every record store in town and invited anyone who worked there who looked cool. Any time we met someone cool we tried to sell him or her a ticket. If he or she refused, we put them on the guest list. The key was to sell a ticket to anyone who would buy a ticket and give tickets to anyone who wouldn't buy a ticket. I even made my mother buy a ticket, but some cute girl in a record store who wouldn't buy a ticket got in free. Sorry, mom.

Then, we sent free tickets and invitations to everyone who worked at the local newspapers. I mean every single person working there got one—it didn't matter if he worked in the mailroom—he got a letter with tickets and an invitation from us. This made a real big impact on the local paper and the people who worked there, and it helped to get an article written about us. I call it the overkill method. You send a letter to everyone, and the people who *never get mail* spread the word to the writers and editors who are too overwhelmed with packages to notice your package. The next thing you know, someone is writing about your group, and the town is buzzing about you.

All this time we thought we were promoting, but we were really networking. Sending invitations to people and asking them to come to see your group is *networking*, and it works like you can't believe. We ended up selling 200 pre-sale tickets, the opening act sold 50 tickets, more than 400 people paid at the door, and just over 100 people showed up from our guest list. All together, we had more than 750 people at our very first show. Now, would you rather play one show every two months to a sold-out crowd or play three or four shows a month to an empty room?

 Sending invitations by mail is a great way to get your band noticed, since most invites are now done via email.

An Empty Venue Kills

I met an amazing person on a road trip, and he changed the way I look at crowds. Over the years, I have seen many outstanding groups play in empty clubs and plenty of bad groups play to sold-out crowds. Until I met this person, I had no idea why. I used to think that a local group's draw had everything to do with their work ethic and quality of their show and music, and to some degree, it does. But the size of a group's following goes much deeper than just willingness to work or promote.

I was in a Starbucks in the middle of New Orleans, interviewing people for a position with our productions company, Gorilla Music. This super-friendly man approached me regarding my company. We got to talking, and he explained his work to me. It changed my understanding of the music business forever.

This person was a public speaker, and he traveled around performing speeches at different high schools. I was amazed when he started to explain his process and the different results he got. Surprisingly, the effectiveness of his presentations was *not based on his performance*, but instead on the *density* of the crowd. He said he would call each school in advance. His only request was that they set up the assembly in a room that would be crowded, based on the number of people who planned to attend. He said that if the school followed his instruction and made sure they used the right-sized room (one in which the students were crowded and everyone sat closely together), then the demonstration would be amazing. Students would participate by raising their hands, asking questions, and laughing at all his jokes. They would all love his presentation. He would get all sorts of compliments and they would ask him back.

On the other hand, if a school didn't follow his directions, and the assembly took place in a larger room where people would spread out, leaving large empty spaces, then his presentation would be a disaster. No one would raise a hand with any questions; no one would laugh at his jokes; and everyone would seem lost and disinterested. This was the *same demonstration* that got huge laughs everywhere else that week…the *same demonstration* that had people captivated the day before.

At this point, I was on the edge of my seat, as excited as you can get in a Starbucks without acting a fool. So I asked him, why would the size or density of the crowd have any impact on the appreciation of the material? It just didn't make sense. As he answered me, I had images in my mind of all these great bands playing in empty rooms. He said, "John, in an empty room, people feel self-conscious and uncomfortable. They become more aware of what *they* are doing than what's happening around them. They feel as if everyone is staring at *them* and that anything *they* do is being noticed and judged. In a room that is full or feels full, everyone feels invisible and uninhibited. Since nobody is noticing them or judging them, they can be themselves. This allows them to focus on the presentation and enjoy it without self-consciousness or awkwardness. If you've ever been to Mardi Gras, you know exactly what I'm talking about."

TIP: If your audience looks disinterested, it might have more to do with the size of the crowd than your performance. By getting them closer to the stage you might be able to regain their attention.

In an instant, everything made sense. I remembered all the times I had seen great bands in empty rooms and had not understood why they couldn't build a following. I remembered thinking to myself, "Wow! No one is here to see this great band." I also remembered that I couldn't wait for those concerts to be over, even if I liked the music. I was bored and uncomfortable at those shows, and I never went back to see most of those great bands. I thought back to all the bands I had seen that I didn't particularly like but that had huge crowds. I came back repeatedly to see them and had fun at their shows, even though I wasn't a fan of their music.

I thought about all the times I played with my first group, Serious Nature, in front of no one. I remembered how awkward I felt on stage performing in a 500-capacity club for twenty or thirty people. If *I* felt awkward, imagine how uncomfortable it was for those thirty people. No wonder they would tell us how great we were and then never return. They may have *thought* we were great and really enjoyed our music, but they didn't enjoy our show because the room felt awkward. No matter how good your group might be, if your fans feel awkward and uncomfortable, they're not going to want to come back.

I remembered all the sold-out shows I played, and how great it felt on stage. That's how your fans feel when you have a great show in a sold-out club. That's what you need to do if you want your fan base to grow— sell out your shows.

I also owned a dance club called Heaven. It was located in a very popular entertainment district called The Flats. The club business is very similar to the business of growing a local group. People go to dance clubs for the same reason they go out to see local groups or concerts: to have fun. Just like the concert business, if the room is crowded people will have fun, tell their friends about the club, and come back again.

When a group of two or more people entered our club, we would over hear them discussing their plans. If we were crowded, they would say things like, "Cool. Let's hang out here!" If we were somewhat busy, but not crowded yet, we would hear conversation like this, "Do you want to check this club out, or should be go somewhere else?" "I don't know. Let's stay for one beer and see what happens." Then, if we were empty, people would walk in the club and turn right around and leave.

It's the same for your fans. If you have strong crowds at your shows, people will have fun, tell their friends about your group, and keeping coming back to see you. If you're playing for small crowds, your fan base will continue to dwindle.

RECAP

- Why are you playing live? Have a good reason.
- Playing a bunch of shows isn't going to grow your fan base.
- To grow your group you need to network aggressively.
- Fans feel more comfortable and have more fun in crowded rooms.
- **To grow your group's draw, pack the venue.**

Grow Your Band Fast

"Call it a clan, call it a **network,** call it a tribe, call it a family;
Whoever you are, you need one."

- Jane Howard

Your Social Circle

So, your group doesn't exist outside of its own social circle, and
you can't use exposure to grow a healthy fan base. What is the
solution? The only effective way to grow an unknown local group's
following is to build a network or a music scene around that group,
person by person. What does it mean to "get out there in the trenches and
drag people to your shows"? It means you have to call everyone you
know and ask them to go to your next show. You have to text the
people you are not comfortable calling, and you have to email everyone
else you know. You have to use your presence on social networking
sites to personally invite people—*the people you know,* but for whom you
don't have phone numbers or direct email addresses. You have to go to
all the places where you might be able to recruit people to come to
your next show. If you wish to grow fast, go a step further; and get

your friends, family, and fans to help you invite even more people to see you play.

Your next show is the only show that matters, because every show afterwards will be affected by the attendance at the next one. It MUST be packed with people who are there to see and hear your group. Preferably, people who run in the same social circles, and have the same interests as your group, musically and otherwise. This event and every other event must be big! Everyone you know should be there.

If this show is not packed, it will be harder to get people out to future shows. Always do everything you can to get your whole social circle out to each show. Make sure everyone in the group gets involved in the process. Even if they're not good at making friends, every little bit helps.

Expand Your Network

OK. You've tapped out your social circle. Now what? The next step is to stretch even further by expanding your social circle beyond its present boundaries. Start looking for more people with similar interests. Make friends at concerts, in bars or clubs, in coffee shops, and in record stores. Make friends everywhere you go, and make friends all the time. For God's sake, make friends with every band you play with and everyone who works in the clubs where you play. This is one of the best ways to expand your fan base, because making friends with another band sometimes means making friends with their entire social circle. Jackpot! When you befriend other bands, you already know you have similar interests, which is an essential component in this process.

Once you find someone with similar interests, see how you can connect with that person. It might be by making great conversation or by helping them in some way. Find a way to enrich his or her life, and you'll be fast friends. Maybe it's as simple as turning them on to your music or finding another cool thing for them to do on a Friday night, like going to your group's show. If it's someone in a band, then the two of you can now start supporting each other's groups by going out to see each other's shows.

> **TIP:** Make friends with 10 bands, and agree to attend each others shows. The average band has 4 members; you just built an instant crowd of 40 people. At their shows, network with all their fans.

My co-author, business partner, and brother, Dan, is better at networking than anyone I know. He seems to know everyone in town. He can't walk down the street without someone saying "hi" to him. Dan loves to talk to people. He likes everyone, and everyone likes him. He's a genuinely friendly guy whom people like the first time they meet him. When he owned Peabody's, he put together a fake band—a group that didn't even play their own instruments. All they did was lip-sink to a recording of cover songs and wear crazy clothes! Most people knew it was a joke, but some thought that it was a real band with real shows. Dan and his friends were so good at networking that they had over a 400-person draw—a 400-person draw for a fake band that played less than three shows a year. If a fake band can build a following, so can you!

I think the reason Dan is so good at networking is that he's always in a great mood. He doesn't think the glass is half full; he thinks the water delivery guy just dropped off a year's supply. That's the kind of attitude that attracts people. Everyone just wants to be around him.

He also has a great memory. Tell him your phone number, and he won't even write down. He just remembers it. Hell, I can't even remember my own phone number! The point is to take an interest in other people; have a fun, upbeat attitude and it's going to be easier to make friends and new fans.

You can and should be networking all the time. In fact, you *must* network all the time if you want to grow your group. If you're in a music store and you see someone buying a Guns N' Roses record and Axl is your favorite singer, just approach that person. Maybe you've even been told that you sound like Axl. In any case, you've just found a networking opportunity. Let this person know about your group, and tell him how Guns N' Rose's has influenced you or your group. Make sure this person knows about your next show, and knows how to find your social networking sites. Business cards or flyers are great for this purpose. I know, I just told you that flyers will not help you promote, and they won't. But they can help you network. Carry them everywhere you go, and use them as a tool to open conversations or to remind fans about your shows. Just don't waste them on telephone poles where they are mostly useless. Finally, try to get this person's information so you can reach him again. If he does give you his contact information, make contact immediately, and try to develop a friendship.

These are the kinds of situations in which you and your whole band need to put yourself on a regular basis. The more often you go to places where you can effectively network and the better you get at networking, the bigger your group's following will become. To a great degree, the size of the network you can create is more important at this stage of your career than almost anything else you can do to create a large following. I have seen it a million times: unpolished groups with large networks that end up with a bigger draw than more experienced and seasoned musicians. Their network and their crowds make their shows more fun for their fans than the groups that have all the experience, but little or no network or fan base.

Be honest for a second. Do you think that people are going to care if the music is the greatest music in the world if they're having a great time at a packed show? The answer is no. If they're having fun, they are going to come back again. On the other hand, if the music is great, but the show sucks and no one is there, are they really going to want to return? They might buy a CD if they love the music, but you won't see them again if the show wasn't any fun.

Think back to a few of your group's most successful shows. Why were those shows successful? Did you spend a lot of money promoting them? Were they successful because you implemented some new promotional tool? Or, were they successful because most of your social circle attended those shows? Most likely it's the latter: your social circle showed up. The groups that can get their social circle out to their shows, write great songs, and put on great shows, grow... and they grow fast. The bands that can't get their social circle out to see them will almost always fizzle out. I have even seen a number of groups grow without great shows or great songs, but I can't remember a single group that has grown a large fan base without a strong social circle, unless they had the help of a radio hit.

Effective Networking

Effective networking includes (1) networking with purpose and (2) networking habitually. Networking with purpose means that you seek out certain people whom you need to meet to help further your career. Networking habitually means that you try to make friends everywhere you go and with every opportunity that arises. I recommend that you include both types of networking in your pursuit of success.

Networking with purpose requires two actions: first, you create a list of needs and wants; and, second, you create a plan. Networking requires friendship and value in order to be effective. If your only objective is to get what you want and move on, you're not going to get very far. The most effective way to network is to bring value to others. If all you do is talk about yourself and ask for favors, people will get turned off very quickly.

If your first goal is to sell out your next show, make a list of everyone your group knows. In fact, make two lists: one list of everyone you think might buy a ticket to your next show and a second list of everyone that will help you sell tickets to your next show. One of the best tools you have is your cell phone. My groups would have band meetings where we would go through our cell phones and call everyone we knew. We would ask everyone to come to our next show. We would go in separate rooms and just start calling. At one meeting, our drummer was a little shy, and he didn't want to invite a certain girl he had in his phone. I grabbed his phone and called her for him. At first, he was mad. The funny thing is that she showed up for the show, and they started dating right after that show. Of course, he forgave me for calling her. The point is, you need to push each other and work hard to get everyone out to your next show. We had great turnouts for those shows, because we put lots of effort into getting our friends to attend.

TIP: It is easier to network if you're in good mood. Try to make other people laugh or find things you have in common with them while networking.

Here is an example of networking with purpose: let's say you need studio time to record your next record, but you don't have any money. Start by calling each studio in town and offering to work or to intern in exchange for studio time. I have not only seen and heard of people getting into a studio this way, but I've done it myself. In more than one instance we were able to record an entire album free of charge. (I discuss how we did this and how you can do it in more detail in Chapter 12, "The Studio.")

Let's say you need a gig. Start by networking with clubs and promoters. It's easy. First, get your group booked, and then do these things: be professional and friendly, and through your conversations with the promoter, try to develop a friendship. Then, bring value to this person. What does the club or promoter need? Clubs want and need to draw people to their venue in order to pay bills, make a profit, and stay in business. So, pack their club for them! If you are friendly, professional, and you pack their club, you'll be on your way to making new friends and valued allies.

A decent club owner or promoter with the right connections can do a lot for you and your group. A friendship with a promoter or club owner can help you to get better shows and better time slots on those shows. Most groups think they are doing the club owner a favor just by performing. It's simply not true. Club owners have hundreds of bands knocking on their doors every day, which means they're doing *you* a favor, no matter how good your group might be.

Every time you go to a club, make friends with the soundman to get a better mix. Make friends with the bartenders to get better service, and make friends with all the customers to increase your draw. Sometimes, befriending a bartender is the fastest way to meet an owner or booking manager; they are usually good friends. To make friends with the bartenders, tip well. When the club is slow, make jokes or find ways to relate to them. When they're busy, respect their time, and stay out of their hair. To make friends with the soundman, respect his time and his talent. Soundmen are disrespected on a daily basis by other bands and drunken patrons. Be the group to acknowledge his or her efforts. Remember, the key to successful networking is to bring value to others. Don't be pushy or fake, and don't drop names or try to act cool.

The same techniques are true of the habitual networker. Be friendly and kind, and be aware of the needs of the people around you. If someone has her hands full, go out of your way to open the door for her, and then make conversation. If she's wearing one of your favorite group's, T-shirts, point out to her how cool she is and how much you love that band. The key is to be honest. How do you act around your friends? You should act the same way around new people. Obviously, you need to be appropriate for the situation, but just being yourself is the best way to start making new friends.

 Use the trunk of your car to carry your band's merchandise. This way you always have your networking tools with you.

Make Your Circle Bigger

Try to network with everyone you meet. The bigger your network of friends, fans, and people directly related to helping your group grow, the better chance you have of succeeding in the music business, and in life. In addition to what I call the habitual networking technique, or networking with everyone you meet, you should also go out of your way to meet people you might not have the opportunity to meet ordinarily. You should also try to meet anyone who likes the same genre of music you write and perform.

But don't stop there! Make a special effort to meet club owners, concert promoters, studio owners, recording engineers, record producers, A&R reps, band managers, talent agents, potential fans, and anyone else who can help your group. Also, try to meet influential people with money, and make friends with all the other groups in town you respect. Make sure you're best friends with the biggest drawing local group in your hometown, and find out *why* they are the biggest group in town. (The reason they're the biggest drawing group in town is because they are good at networking.) Learn everything you can from everyone in your network. Become a sponge and suck in information from everyone around you.

How do you meet these people just outside your social circle? The same way you grow your fan base. Start with people you know or who are easy to reach. Book that first gig, and ask the club owner how many people you need to draw in order for him to be impressed enough to have you back as a headliner. Just by asking this question, you will be miles ahead of most of the groups that club owner books. You see, most bands try to impress promoters and club owners with how talented they think they are or how great they perform. Unfortunately, talent doesn't pay the bills; customers pay the bills. If you talk to a club owner on his level, showing him that you understand his real needs, he will appreciate you for it. You will also be demonstrating to him that you're more sophisticated than most groups that do not understand his position or the music business.

Over Deliver

Make sure you undersell your performance! That's right, you read it correctly! If your group can sell 200 tickets or walk up 200 people, then tell the club owner you can get 100-125 people there. Almost every band in this country *over* sells. They tell club owners that they have a 250-person draw, when they can't walk up ten people. If they're good, they think they are great, and they let everyone know about it. Don't make the same mistakes. Once you make promises you can't keep, you become the exaggerating band with a huge ego that made an unfulfilled promise.

Instead, you should under-promise and over-deliver every time you guarantee something. Tell the club owner you can bring one hundred people to his club, and then bring two hundred people or even three hundred. If your music is great, let it speak for itself. I can't begin to tell you about all the groups that told me they had two hundred fans and then brought fewer than 10 people to my club. Guess what happened to them the next time they asked me for a gig? That's right—no gig!

Find and Meet VIPs

Once you have delivered a few hundred people to the club and started to build a rapport with the club owner, and everyone else associated with the club, it is time to start asking them for help. I promise you, if you bring two hundred people to a club, they will want to do whatever they can to help you and your group. They will recognize that your group has potential, and they will want to make friends with you as much as you want to make friends with them. Clubs only make money if a group can bring people in. So, once you position your group as one that can bring lots of people, it's time to let them return the favor. First, ask everyone at the club for advice. Ask them how you can get more people to your shows. (This is a great place to start since it also benefits the club financially). Then, try to find out who knows whom and what they can do to help further your career; for example, do they know anyone from record labels or talent agencies?

 Once your band has a big draw, begin asking venues for favors. Start by asking for advice on how to get an even bigger crowd to their venue. This will open the door for even more favors.

When I owned my own concert club, I talked with talent agents daily and knew people at different record labels. Every club that books national talent is in the same position. Start finding out whom and what they know. Most club owners go to different conferences annually; one of the biggest is South by Southwest in Austin, Texas. Get familiar with it, as well as other conferences. Try to go to one of these events with a club owner, promoter, or some other VIP. While you're there, make friends with influential people, and network with everyone you can every step of the way.

Start applying for every festival performance you can find on the Internet. If someone from a record company is going to be there, you have to try to get your group on the bill. The point is to position yourself in a place where you can increase the size of your network with people who can help you. The company we own—Gorilla Music—holds festivals around the country specifically for unsigned artists. We usually fly in A&R scouts or other VIPs. All of these groups should be trying hard to network with these people, but in reality only a few even approach them. These scouts are people just like you are, and most of them are very nice. Remember, they wouldn't have come if they didn't want to help people. So, they are very approachable, and you need to network with these people. Introduce yourself, tell them about your group; ask them to check you out live or listen to your music. Then, put on a great show, and never lose sight of the bigger picture: you are trying to get to know the movers and shakers, the people who can help you the most with your career. It takes a little research and work to network properly, but it will save you time and money and get you to the top much faster than anything else.

RECAP

- Networking is just another word for making new friends.

- Expand your social circle beyond its present boundaries. Make friends everywhere you go, and make friends all the time.

- To network effectively you must create value for others.

- Effective networking includes networking with purpose and networking habitually.

- Get familiar with VIPs, and know where to find them.

STEP 2:
Create and Put On
OUTSTANDING SHOWS

Make Your Shows Amazing

"I was impressed by Hendrix. His attitude was brilliant.
Even the way he walked was amazing."

- Ritchie Blackmore

Eliminate the Ugliness

If you're going to perform live, you need to make your performances impressive and entertaining. When most bands prepare for a gig, they run through their songs one at a time, stopping in-between songs to check that everyone knows his or her parts. They try to make sure each song sounds tight and professional. Sometimes they even write a new song or come up with ideas to make their show better or more interesting. Very few groups put any effort into anything else, which is too bad. With a little more planning and effort, most groups could get much further.

When you run through your songs one at a time, stopping after each one to discuss how it sounded and to decide what to play next, you are creating bad habits. This dead time between songs will surely end up affecting your performance the night of your show. This is the area where most local groups fail. They get up on stage and take what seems like a lifetime between songs. They tune their instruments, talk, and awkwardly make inside jokes that no one in the audience understands. It's unprofessional, and even worse, it's boring. Frankly, rehearsing one song at a time has not only created this problem, but reinforced it.

TIP: Rehearse the breaks between your songs. Fans get bored when they have to wait too long for your next song to start.

Rehearse like professionals. When you practice for live performances, use the dress rehearsal method. Play your set from start to finish without stopping. Take the time to figure out what's going to happen between songs, and practice that. On the night of your show, you do not have to repeat everything exactly as rehearsed, but you should try to get a feel for how much time will elapse between songs, and prepare accordingly. What happens between your songs is an important part of your show. I know you need to get ready for your next song, but what does your audience do while you're preparing? Are you going to let them sit there bored? If you take two to three minutes after each song to prepare for the next, you're going to lose their attention.

Before you start dress rehearsals, I recommend that you rehearse the beginnings and endings of each song. To do this effectively, play the last part of your first song. Then practice what you're going to do before the next song starts. Immediately play the first part of the next song, and stop. You should play about thirty seconds of each song. Then repeat the process with the end of the second song and the beginning of the third song and so on. By rehearsing in this way, you'll improve your shows and enhance your fans' experience by eliminating the ugliness that occurs between songs.

Dance club DJs are taught to eliminate all gaps between songs. They even change tempos to match beats between adjoining songs. When done properly the crowd never leaves the dance floor. When an inexperienced DJ makes the mistake of putting breaks between songs, the crowd leaves the dance floor like a tornado's coming! Inexperienced bands make the same mistake. People leave the floor because it's uncomfortable to stand there and watch nothing happen. As the crowd's focus turns away from the performance, everyone become uncomfortable. Keep the focus on your group, and people will be relaxed. Make sure you keep the silence, the guitar tuning, and anything else that will make your audience uncomfortable to a minimum.

Spontaneity

Most people believe spontaneity cannot be rehearsed. Some even believe that being well rehearsed will get in the way of having a wild, spontaneous performance. That kind of thinking is way off. I realize that this sounds like an oxymoron: the better prepared your group, the more likely it is that you'll have a creative, spontaneous performance.

Understand that your confidence level is higher when you are well rehearsed. You do not have to focus as much of your attention on your performance, leaving you free to imagine and create. An unrehearsed group needs to spend their energy making sure they remember their parts. They need to concentrate on everything that they're going to do while they're performing. If you're not sure what's about to happen, or what song's next, then you're going to be under-prepared. When you're under-prepared, you become too preoccupied with your performance to create any spontaneous moments. So, the more you rehearse, the better chance you have of finding great impromptu moments on stage. The high of a great performance will create even more spontaneous moments.

TIP: Always have a few things planned in the event of technical difficulties. That way, if there is a problem, you won't lose the audiences' attention.

Important Preparations

Have you timed your songs? Do you know how long your set is for your upcoming show? These are important issues. You will have a problem if, with three songs left, the soundman starts cuing you, "last song." Time your songs and your set, and know what's going to happen during and in between songs. Preparing for the stage is not difficult. Have a few topics or cool things prepared to discuss in case you have technical difficulties or some other unforeseen problem. The point is to be prepared.

Pack Your Shows

Remember the guy I met at Starbucks who went around from school to school performing demonstrations? Remember the dance hall patrons that turned around and left when our dance club was empty? These lessons taught me the importance of performing in a crowded room, and what happens when you play in empty one. The most important thing you can do to make your shows entertaining is to pack the venue with enthusiastic people. It's more important to your fans than anything else. Everyone wants to have a good time, and filling the room is the best way to ensure that your fans enjoy themselves. Remember, until people know your music and like your music, they're not there just to hear your music. Yes, having good songs is an important factor, but it's not the *only* factor—not until you see crowds of people in the audience singing along to your songs.

After showing them a good time, the next best way to get people interested in your music is by making a genuine connection with them.

TIP: Try to schedule your shows in the right sized venues. It's always better to play a smaller room and fill it up than a bigger room and leave it empty.

Connect With Your Audience

Work hard to get people to your shows. If you do, you will minimize the number of shows you play to an empty room. But if you do find your group in a situation where the room *is* empty, then try to create the illusion of a large crowd. Ask the crowd, however small, to get closer to the front of the stage so the room appears to be packed with people. As you do this, you will see an instant rise in the audience's appreciation of your group. Almost immediately, your energy level on stage will also increase. Do this even in a full room. Always get the people as close to the stage as possible. Ask everyone you know to come straight to the stage the second you start playing. If you can get thirty or more people to approach the stage simultaneously as your set begins, other people will follow like sheep. People feel uncomfortable not following the herd. When they see a room full of people moving towards the front of the stage, they will follow. I guarantee it.

> **TIP:** The closer people are to the stage, the more they will enjoy your performance. Use different approaches throughout your show to keep asking the crowd to get closer to you.

At one of our festivals, I hosted a free seminar designed to help groups. We scheduled everyone to check in for the event and held the seminar the same day. Since there were hundreds of bands, we created a second seminar and check-in date for the groups that couldn't make it to the first seminar. The first seminar was packed, and my presentation went extremely well. At the second seminar, there were only a few dozen people in attendance, and the room felt empty. It *wasn't* going very well. I was ill-at-ease, and so was the audience. No one was paying much attention. It was just as the guy from New Orleans had explained to me. Since the crowd was small the room felt empty and uncomfortable. This discomfort made my presentation less entertaining.

I waited until the part of the presentation where I talked about that guy from New Orleans. I discussed what I learned about the effects of crowds and the effects of empty rooms. Right at that point, I got down off the stage and asked everyone to pull their chairs together around me. Once we were all in a tight circle, I continued the presentation, and the atmosphere changed instantly. The same people who were bored and preoccupied ten minutes ago became captivated, and everyone relaxed. It ended up becoming one of my best seminars ever. Afterwards, everyone wanted to meet me and talk to me about his or her group.

Again, if you ever find yourself in this situation, take the microphone and ask everyone in the club to get as close to the stage as possible. This technique allows people the opportunity to pay attention to your show, which gives them the chance to enjoy it. It will also help you to make a connection with your crowd. At the local level, you need to do everything you can to get people involved in your show. Making a connection with your crowd is one of the best ways to get people wanting to come back to see you. Get them clapping, singing, or moshing to your music. Do everything you can to get people active, and they're ten times more likely to come back. Frankly, the act of moshing is one of the reasons local metal bands have a much easier time growing a fan base. Alternative or soft rock groups that don't have an activity to help them connect with their fans have a much harder time.

Participation Leads to Appreciation

If the only thing your fans can do is stand there and listen, they are less likely to feel like a part your scene. Think about it. Most of them aren't familiar with your music yet. So, what are they going to do? Once people become participate in a concert in some active way, they become a bigger part of the show. This helps them feel more connected to your band. If you can make people feel like they're a part of your music scene, they will be more likely to come more often to see you perform. Try getting them to chant, dance, or laugh and you're going to be ahead of the game. As listeners, we tend to be less active participants, and that can lead us to become disinterested in a subject. If you can get the audience engaged in an activity that requires their participation, the chance of them enjoying your show goes up dramatically.

Other ways to connect with your fans is by selling them T-shirts or CDs, getting them to sign up for your email list, or just by having a real conversation with them after your show. Interact with your fans as much as possible; the more you can do to connect with them, the more likely it is that they will have a great time and come back. Having a fan buy a CD or shirt from you is an activity, just like getting them to clap, mosh, or dance. Any activity you can get an audience member involved in will enhance his or her experience. That's right: if they buy your T-shirt they will like you better, because they got the chance to do something with you. There is a chapter later in the book on T-shirts that will change how your group feels about merchandise. So, remember to fill the room, or at least make it feel full by gathering everyone to the front of the stage. Then find ways to connect with your audience.

TIP: Use a gimmick to get fans involved in your shows. One band I know passes out wigs and hats to get their fans more involved in their performances.

Sound

Most reputable clubs will provide sound, lights, and a decent soundman. In some situations, they will also provide someone to run the lights. Some groups choose to bring their own sound man. This is great if he or she is very experienced, familiar with your material, familiar with the club's equipment, and free or very affordable. This is not usually the case. Fortunately, most house sound engineers are very capable of mixing pretty much any group. They know the room and the house sound system better than anyone a local group could afford.

For these reasons, I highly recommend using the house engineer and saving your money for something else. The only problem you might have is that you're going to run into a lot of moody soundmen.

Moody Sound-Men

Have you ever wondered why so many soundmen are crabby or difficult? I believe it is because they have the most stressful job in the business. Look at what they go through on a nightly basis: they're dealing with sometimes as many as ten groups, all with different concerns and requests. Some of these groups have over-inflated egos and trouble following directions. It's always the club's manager or the promoter who tells the sound person what the schedule is for the night. Then, they have bands that show up late or refuse to get off stage on time. Sometimes, groups are downright rude about a schedule, over which the soundman has no control. Almost every night some drunken patron tries to tell him how to do his job. At the end of the night, at least one band member or fan will inevitably tell him how he sucks as a soundman or yells at him for cutting them off after forty-five minutes, when they were scheduled to play thirty. Rarely does anyone thank him for a job well done.

At the local level, you do not need to bring your own soundman to your shows. Instead, you need to start the day by giving the soundman the respect he deserves. I recommend the first thing you do when you arrive at the club is to say "hi" to the soundman. Ask him his name and whether he needs you to do anything. Better yet, find out his name before you even get there by calling the club in advance. Tell him you'll be available when he needs you, and thank him. If you really want to make an impression, bring him his favorite sandwich or soft drink. Again, you can probably find this out in advance by calling the club. Once you make the soundman your friend, he will go the extra mile for you.

Bring the sound-man a soft drink from the bar, and let him know that he's doing a great job. He has as much control over how good you sound as you do, so it's important that he likes you.

Stage Volume Impact

Did you know that your stage volume has a huge impact on the way that your group is going to sound to the audience? By "stage volume impact," I mean how loud you turn up your amps on stage will affect what comes out of the front of the PA system. The louder your amps are on stage, the less the soundman can do to adjust your sound out of the front of the PA. I am amazed by the number of groups that turn their amps up all the way on stage and then do not understand why no one can hear their singer. Try to look at it this way: your guitars are actually being amplified twice, once with your amp, and then through the PA. The vocals are only being amplified once, through the PA.

Based on the type of music you play and what your main concerns might be, a louder stage volume might be priority number one. For you, the sound coming out of the front speakers might take a backseat to increased energy levels. A louder stage volume tends to increase the energy levels on stage and out front, for the crowd. You need to be able to control your volume to get the results you want on any particular night. It takes awareness and practice. I suggest you find a happy medium that can provide you the energy you need on stage, while allowing the best possible mix out front.

Be a little strategic if you have a guitarist who needs to be extremely loud to get the right energy and sound from his amp. If his amp is drowning everyone else out, try turning his amp away from the front of the stage. This way he can maintain his energy level, and the soundman can still get a good mix. The louder your drums and amps are, the harder it is going to be to hear the vocals out front. For some groups, like hardcore metal groups that have more of a scream-type vocal, that might be just what you what they want, and that's just fine.

Other things to think about are properly tuned guitars and well-tuned drums. You want all the guitars to have new strings, but not brand-new strings. If they're too new they can easily go out of tune while you're on stage. A few days old (depending on how often you play) should be fine. If you play three hours a day, every day, then three-month-old strings are not going to cut it. Make sure you know how to properly string your instruments and how to stretch your strings. Most music stores can help you in these areas, if you're unsure.

Lights Are Critical

One of my favorite subjects is lighting. Most clubs have lights, but no light person. You can teach almost anyone in about five minutes how to run lights for you, and you can usually get a friend to help for free. At the local level, your lights are as important as your sound. Lights can make your shows so much better for your fans. They can help make you look like a national act and increase the energy level on stage and within the crowd. Lighting is so easy to do; yet, no one does it. Most groups don't even think about the lights. The soundman turns them on and leaves up whatever scene (group of lights) happens to be in the board at the time. Most lighting systems are simple. They have about six to ten scenes that all turn on and off at the same time with the push of a button. They have single faders (individual lights) on a switch that can turn on or off or be brightened or dimmed by the operator's control panel.

I have found that the best light shows are all about movement. It's not so much what you do with the lights. It's more about creating some kind of movement on stage with the lights. Try mixing in some scene lighting by moving from one scene to another with your song. Then mix in a very mild strobe effect by slightly turning the individual faders up and down, dimming several lights at the same time. Again, it's really just about doing *something* with them.

> **TIP:** Rent or buy some floor cans for your next show. When you introduce the crowd to new lights, it makes your show superior to other shows seen in that venue.

Here is the key to really looking professional. It's so simple, and no one will even realize that you're doing it. It's almost subliminal. Most national acts do this, but very few local groups do it. It's called a black out, and you do exactly that. You simply black out the stage for about two seconds in between songs. Then you have the light person turn them up a little so the band can see just enough to prepare for the next song. If the next song starts with a quiet guitar, put a little light on that person. After it gets loud again use a little more or a lot more light. The lights should help the music speak to the crowd almost like a story. The great thing about lights is how they affect everyone in the room, including the members of the group. I promise you, the better your light show, the higher the energy level will be in the room and on stage.

A few years ago, I was working with a band that was scheduled to play a club I used to own. They had played this club many times before, and the soundman had mixed them before. This was their first show there since I started working with them. I told them to bring a friend along so I could teach him or her to run the lights. I taught that person how to create movement on the stage by moving the lights around, and how to black out the stage between songs.

Three or four songs into the set, the soundman turned to me and said, "This group's great. Are they a national act?" When I told him who they were, he was shocked. He said, "Wow. I didn't even recognize them. They sound great tonight!" In reality, they didn't sound any different than the last time they played. They were a talented, tight group of players. The soundman just wasn't used to seeing local groups act like professionals, so they got his attention. He actually listened to their songs instead of blocking them out, which is what most soundmen do after mixing a few thousand groups.

Creating Energy on Stage

Do you know what helps a light show more than anything else? Smoke! A smoky room will make the light show much more defined. When the stage has a layer of smoke on it, the light rays become much more prominent. For a lot of groups a smoke machine might not fit their group's image. However, I'm not suggesting that groups use a smoke machine to create a typical smoke machine effect or to turn their show into some kind of Kiss concert. It can be used that way, but what I'm talking about is creating a very thin layer of smoke so that no one can even detect a smoke machine. I had a smoke machine in a dance club I owned, and no one ever knew we even had it or that we used it every single night. It made the club more fun because of the movement it created. The human eye is attracted to movement, and smoke helps to define light rays, making them easier to see.

Sectional Rehearsals = Tightness

In order to get tighter and better prepared, you need to schedule sectional rehearsals. A sectional rehearsal is when just the drummer and bass player get together to practice the set, or the guitarist and bass player get together, and so on. Getting any two or three members rehearsing the set, as apposed to the entire group, forces everyone to know the material better. It also gives the group another perspective on its songs. Sometimes, you'll find that two instruments that sounded OK as a group actually sound bad together. You find that those two instruments have been drowning each other out, masking the problem.

Stage Presence

The way you look and act on stage is just as important as how you sound. You should record every song you have from the start to finish and review it. That's not all; you should also videotape rehearsals and live performances to see what you look like while you're performing. Often, the club will have a recording device for you to use, and sometimes they can even videotape it (usually for a charge). However, if those options are not available, bring your own recording device and video recorder, and have a friend tape your show.

Recording and videotaping your performance can help you get a better perspective of what's really happening on stage. When you're in the moment, things tend to appear either better or worse than they really are. By recording the event, it gives you the ability to see and hear your performance from a spectator's point of view. As a group, you can sit down and evaluate your performance together. Any time you can see yourself from another viewpoint you can learn new things about yourself and your performance. Any time you learn something new, you grow as a person and as a musician. Recording your shows is a must if you're serious about your musical career. Sports teams watch their games to improve. You too should record and watch every live show you play, so you can improve.

 Use more than one recording device to record your next show. By doing this, you will get different perspectives on your groups sound.

   A video or audio recording of your performance can really give you some insight on all the areas of your performance that may need work. Also, watch the audience. This can help you determine what your audience seems to enjoy the most about your shows. You honestly look and sound much different than you think you do as each event takes place. You need to see and hear your performances from the same perspective as your fans do. While you're up on stage in the moment and your adrenalin running, you can't get a realistic assessment of your actual performance. Without accurate information, how can you improve what you do on stage? So, record and video tape all your shows. Then, spend some time reviewing each tape. Look for the good, the bad, and the ugly; improve what you do for your next show.

   Lastly, watch what you do between songs. Nothing is worse at a show than dead air. If you rehearse entire shows, and plan segues or black outs between songs, you'll keep the audience entertained through your entire performance. Your show will be amazing!

RECAP

- When you practice for live performances, play your set from start to finish without stopping.

- Time your songs and your set, and know what's going to happen during and in between songs.

- Connect and interact with your fans as much as possible.

- Soundmen have the most stressful job in the business; give them the respect they deserve.

- Lights can help make you look like a national act and increase the energy level on stage and inside the venue.

- A smoky room will make the light show much more defined.

- Audio and videotape your performance to see your group from the audience's perspective.

Book Your Shows Properly

"Book your shows at least 6-8 weeks apart, or prepare to fail."

- Dan Cull

One Show at a Time

Does your group have a following of about thirty to fifty fans? If so, you're like most other groups in your area. If you have more than fifty, you're doing pretty well. If you have more than 100, you're doing great. Unfortunately, most groups' fan bases have a tendency to decline when they ought to be growing. In large part, this has to do with over-exposure in the marketplace, but it goes much deeper than simply playing out too much in your hometown. While over exposure is often the cause, it is the *effect* that is truly responsible for bands losing fans. When a band performs more than one show in the same market within a short space of time, it splits its fan base in half or in thirds if it has three concerts in the same town in one month.

In Chapter Two, I explained why groups should not rely on the exposure method to grow their local following. The exposure method is when groups try to get booked on every show they can in order to expose more people to their group and their music. The most effective way to grow a local group's following is through proper planning. It's very important to space your shows out far enough, so that your events always seem special. Never let your fans know of more than one opportunity at a time in the same market to see your group perform.

> **TIP:** Secretly plan all your group's shows for the year. This way you'll always be prepared for your next show.

If you check out the average local group's social networking sites, you'll see all of their upcoming shows listed—usually two to three shows—all within a one or two-month period. Bands do this to give their fans plenty of notice, hoping to entice them to come out to their shows. There are two problems with this scenario: first, you should never give your local fans more than one opportunity to see you at any time. Second, it takes six to eight weeks to promote a show properly through networking. If you have more than one show in a six-week period, you tend to split your draw between those shows. Half of your crowd comes to one show, and the other half to the second show.

How many times have you heard a fan say, "I can't make it this Friday to see your group, but I will be there next Saturday"? If you have heard someone say this, you've made a huge mistake—the biggest mistake a group can make when trying to develop a local following. One of the main reasons people go to local shows is to have fun by meeting or mingling with other like-minded people. If you divide your crowd in half, then half of the cool people your fans were hoping to hang out with won't be there. Your fans at the first show won't know that your other fans are going to be at your next show. When you gave them a choice of shows by announcing all your shows at once, they chose the most convenient one. That thirty-person draw now appears to be a fifteen-person draw to everyone at each show, which will look pretty pitiful to your fans, the other groups, and to the clubs where you're trying to get booked again.

At the same time, you're creating too much supply. Your friends and fans can't come see your group three or four times a month. What if your favorite group came to town and played at your local arena every night of the week for six months? How many shows would you attend? After paying for admission, parking, drinks, and everything else, could you really afford to see more than a couple of shows? If they perform the same show every night, wouldn't that get boring after a few shows? Most of the bands I asked this question to agree that they would go to only one, maybe two shows. So, why do so many groups play out so often?

Hey, I was guilty of using the exposure method, even though our group kept getting worse and worse results each time we performed, and our local draw continued to dwindle. We loved playing out, so it was hard to control ourselves. When an opportunity came our way, we would grab it. It wasn't until I left that first group, and started creating plans to build a following for my second group, that things changed. Once I spent the time and effort to work on one show at a time, my new group built a following practically overnight!

If you want to grow a huge fan base, book one show every six to eight weeks, and only announce one show at a time. Network like crazy every day, and make sure everyone in your group is getting the word out to their friends and contacts. Then, make every show an event and as much fun as possible, so that your fans can't wait for your next show.

8 Weeks Apart

It takes at least six weeks to network a show properly. Once you confirm a date, it takes a few days just to gather the information you need about the show, the venue, and everything else. Then, it takes time for all the members to obtain tickets or flyers to use as networking tools. It takes time to get the word out, to be sure your fans know about the show. As a promoter and former club owner, I know from experience that any show booked less than six weeks in advance will suffer.

The proper way to book your shows is to space them out at least six weeks apart, or longer, if possible. You should have future shows confirmed and ready to promote. It's important that the night of that first show, you announce the next show while you have your fans all in one place. Have flyers designed and ready for the next show, but wait until that night to release those flyers. Every time you play, you should be announcing your next local show. Don't do it sooner, or you'll be competing with yourself and increasing your supply, which always depletes demand. Book one show at a time, and give yourself enough time to network each show properly. You'll start seeing better results right away.

 Always have your flyers designed for your next event months in advance, but wait until the night of your first show to distribute them.

Use All Your Efforts

Once you have control of your bookings, and you are properly spacing your shows out, it's time to focus hard on that next show. Use all your effort to get as many people out to see you as possible. Make sure that everyone in the group is working hard at networking. Try to get as many people to help you as possible. Get friends and family to help you network by selling tickets and passing out flyers and other promotional materials. Spend every day telling people about your group and your upcoming show. Create a plan and a make a list of everyone you can tell about your show and another list of people who can or will help you network. Stay on top of your plan to make sure everyone on your list knows about your show and is helping you promote it.

If you work hard to get everyone you know to your first few shows, and you put on a great one with great songs, the scene will start to build itself. If you wait around for someone else to build it for you, it will never happen. The harder you work on those first few shows and the more effective you are, the easier it will be for you to get people to your shows in the future.

Create a Scene

Throughout most of my twenties and early thirties, when I was single, I went out all the time to clubs and bars. As discussed earlier, I went to see some groups I wasn't particularly fond of musically, and I didn't put much thought into to it, either. I would catch a group playing locally, and if I had fun and met some cool people or a cute girl at one of their shows, I would go back to see them again. I was hoping to see the same people or even a few new people. My friends and I did this all the time.

Your first show is your most important show. You will not get a second chance to make a first impression. Make your first show impressive in every way.

Sometimes, a friend of mine or I would suggest seeing a local group that neither of us cared much for. If we liked the crowd that was following them, we would go to see them often. These were groups that had large followings and played about one show every other month, and it was fun. These groups had successfully created a scene around themselves, and it was paying off big for them. That's what your group needs to do: build a big music scene around your band, so other people start following you just to be a part of that scene. This is key to growing your group locally.

RECAP

- Most fan bases have a tendency to decline when they ought to be growing. In large part, this has to do with over exposure in the marketplace.

- If you want to grow a huge fan base, book one show every six to eight weeks, and only announce one show at a time.

- You should have future shows confirmed and ready to promote, so the night of that first show, you can announce the next one while you have your fans all in one place.

- One of the keys to growing locally is to build a big enough following that people start following you just to join your scene.

Sell-Out Your Shows

"Since the beginning, it was just the same.
The only difference, the crowds are bigger now."

-Elvis Presley

The Right Venue

Booking your shows in properly-sized venues is critical. You don't want something too small or, even worse, something too big. Playing a show in a venue that feels half-empty will make the experience awkward for everyone. Try to pick a cool room that you and your fans already frequent—one that you're sure you can sell out easily.

Once you've picked out the right venue, make sure to pick the right date. Choose a date at least six weeks out. Two months or more in advance is even better. Then, once you have the venue and the date, create a plan to sell out your show.

The 100 Person Rule

Through my experience, both as musician and a club owner, I have been able to recognize that groups with draws over 100 people tend to grow. Groups with draws under 100 people tend to shrink. As a booking agent, knowing this rule, I have implemented bonus structures for groups that can bring 100 or more people to their shows. I understand that if a band can reach that 100 person mark, they will begin to develop in their market.

Believe it or not, getting 100 people to your shows is *easy*—as long as you are not over-saturating the market with shows. Look in your phone, and count how many contacts you have. If everyone in your group called every person in their phone, how many people would you be able to get to your shows? Or, if everyone in your group emailed every one of their contacts, how many people could you get to see you? What if everyone in your group got at least five family members or close friends to come with them, how many people would that be? Now, how many people would that be in total? Are you really asking everyone you know to come to your shows? I am sure there's room for improvement.

Selling Tickets Made Easy

When selling tickets, the first thing you need is a plan. Start by having a group meeting and making a few key lists. The first list should include all the people who might help you sell tickets. Make sure you include close friends, cool family members, cool co-workers and anyone else who might be willing to help. You want to find individuals who are going to be able to sell tickets to people that might like or at least appreciate your music. Try to figure out how many tickets each of these people might be able to sell, and then contact each one of them and ask for their help.

Years ago, Dan was helping a local artist named *Jackie* with one of her shows. He shared this strategy with her. She was able to get over 50 people to help her sell tickets for one of her shows. She successfully sold *over 250 tickets* to that performance. After that show, her group became local *headliners* and a musical staple in their market.

Your next list should include all the people who might buy a ticket. Figure out how you're going to reach each one of them, via phone, email or Facebook. Make sure everyone in your group participates; the more help you have, the bigger your results. Remember, the more people you get to each show, the faster future shows will grow on their own, and the less internal effort you will need down the road.

Once you get a few hundred people to each of your shows that enjoy your music, you will have created a scene around your group. That scene will take on a life of its own, and your fan base will start growing on its own. Now the day of the show, make sure you get contact information from every person who bought a ticket. Try to get their names, email addresses, social networking addresses, and phone numbers, if possible.

Mass text messaging is another effective tool to remind others of your shows, especially once you have gone beyond pre-sale tickets. One of the most popular bartenders and musicians I know is the king of texting. On the day of one of his shows, or anytime he is bartending, he sends everyone he knows text messages to remind them about his event. Since he is so popular—probably as a result of his personality and his relentless texting—he always draws big crowds. His bands are some of the most popular in town. He is so popular that when my brother Dan and I bought in to another club last year, we asked him to become partners on it with us. That club is successful today, in large part, due to his popularity.

Graduating From Pre-Sale Tickets

It is important to graduate beyond pre-sale tickets as fast as possible, but only once your band is truly ready for it. You will know your band is ready once your fans start coming to you for tickets, instead of the other way around. This usually happens around the time you start averaging more than 100 people for every show. When your band reaches that kind of draw, you will probably be able to count on having enough walk ups to fill the rest of the venue.

If you've been in the same band for 2-1/2 years and you still have to pre-sell tickets to get people to your shows, then you're probably doing something wrong. Maybe you haven't gotten enough people out to your shows, so your fans are not having fun. Maybe you're playing too often in your home market, or maybe your music or your live shows still need work. Whatever the case may be, it's crucial for you to be your own toughest critic, so you can figure out what you're doing wrong and what you can do to change it.

Last year, Dan observed multi-platinum music producer *Jeff Blue* deliver a consultation with a band that was unable to critique their own music in a reasonable fashion. They crowded into to a car together, where the group played a few songs for Jeff and Dan. As the band members played their material for Jeff and Dan, one member started skipping parts of their songs. He kept explaining that the next part of the song was better. Jeff asked this member if these were the best songs that they could produce. This band member insisted that he was proud of each song as-is. Jeff pointed out that these could not be the best songs possible, or he would not have skipped so much of each song.

It's important to be honest with yourself, to know when your songs need work and when they are ready. It's important to be real about your work ethic, and to realize that the music business is not an *impossible* dream—but it's also not easy either. If you want to succeed, you're going to have to work hard.

My group, The AKT, always worked hard. We did such an amazing job on our first show—by selling 200 tickets and walking up over 400 people—that we never had to sell tickets again. However, we also worked hard on everything else; we had an amazing, entertaining show, and great music. We were able to get college radio airplay, a lot of press, and impressed people to the point where they looked up to us, musically speaking. We created a huge buzz and a great scene around our band, and it all started with us networking our butts off.

> **TIP:** Visualize your group's goals as if you have already achieved them. If your first goal is to sell out a certain venue, picture a sold out crowd and a marquee that says "sold-out" on it.

Selling Tickets to a Funeral

For years, we've had bands who sell 100 tickets tell us how easy it is. They tell us their friends are excited to buy tickets, and that their fans actually seek them out. We've also had bands that have worked really hard and sold less than 20 tickets. Most of *them* told us how hard it was to sell tickets. They told us how no one wanted to buy them. Sometimes, they said people complained that the tickets were too expensive, there were too many or not enough groups on the bill, the show's going to start too late or too early, or some other lame excuse.

When we first noticed this—groups with the highest sales telling us how easy it was for them and groups with the least ticket sales complaining about the difficulty of selling tickets—we were confused. Honestly, we just chalked it up to work ethic, but as I explained to you in Chapter Two, it goes much deeper than just work ethic or talent. It really comes down to the fact that people don't like to go to poorly attended shows because it's uncomfortable, boring, and feels awkward.

The groups that sell five or ten tickets to their shows are selling a dreadful time to their friends. I call it "selling tickets to a funeral." When a group plays for an empty room, it can feel as awkward as a funeral for everyone there. Also, it's a lot like your group's funeral, because those people who actually came out to see you will probably never see you again. On the other hand, groups that sell 100 or more tickets to their shows are selling tickets to a *party*.

Picture this: you buy a ticket to a friend's concert, you get there, he hits the stage, and the room's empty. It's like you and a dozen other people in the room. You're trying to pay attention to your friend's group, but the only thing you can think about is how *uncomfortable* you are—you feel like everyone's staring at you in this empty room. After the show, your friend asks how it was. Of course you say it was great, but frankly, you can't wait to leave. Two days later, there's your friend asking you to buy a ticket to his next show. What are you going to do? My guess is, you're going to come up with some lame excuse as to why you can't come to his show.

Now picture this: a friend sells you a ticket to his show, you get there, the room is packed and people are cheering as your friend's group hits the stage. You can't believe how crowded it is and how good the band is. There are people all other the place—both people you know, and people that you would like to know. Your friend gets off the stage and before he can ask what you thought, you tell him that his group is amazing and he smiles. Just talking to him makes you feel like a celebrity, and you can see everyone watching the two of you talk. Does this help you understand why it's easier to sell 100 tickets than 20 tickets?

Get The Town Buzzing

Once your group can bring at least 100 people to every show, people will start talking about your group. The club owners and other promoters will want you on their shows. The bartenders will become familiar with your group and they will start wanting to work your shows; security guards and soundmen will know of you and the town will start to talk.

Get 100 people to your shows and other groups are going to want to play with your group. Get 200 people to your shows and people in nearby cities will start to hear about you and consider booking you. You'll even start to draw people out to those shows. Other local groups will start begging to play on your shows. Getting other groups interested in playing with your band is huge. One of the groups that Dan used to book at Peabody's was called 13 Faces. They were so popular with the other local bands in town that even though they were only worth about $500, based on their draw, Dan paid them $1,500 a show. Other groups in town were so in love with this band that they would work their asses off to bring a crowd. These bands wanted their fans to know that they were playing with 13 Faces. That effort translated into sold out shows, allowing 13 Faces to receive payment based on their indirect draw, and based on their popularity with the other local groups.

Fliers Don't Work?

That's right: flyers don't work. Here we go again, right? You're probably thinking, "What is he talking about? Everyone uses flyers to promote their shows." You're right. Flyers are the number one technique groups use to promote their shows… but they don't work! At least not in the way they have been used in the past—as a promotional tool. Remember, your group doesn't exist outside of its own social circle, and if you're networking effectively, then everyone you know should already be aware of your next show.

Fliers are useful tools, but they cannot be used to promote your group or your shows. They can, however, be used to help you create name recognition and to help you network. One of the best ways to use flyers is as a networking tool. Head out to every show in town, or any place in town where people who like the kind of music you play hang out. Bring your flyers and tickets with you, and introduce yourself to everyone there. Tell them about your group and your upcoming show. It's good to point to your flyer to get their attention, and then hand it to them, making eye contact with them as you do.

If you're in a metal band that's influenced by Metallica, then make sure that, when they come to town, you're at their concert and you're networking with everyone. Yes, hand out flyers as you talk to people, make friends with them, and tell them about your group. Explain that Metallica is one of your biggest influences. If you network with people as you hand out flyers, you increase the likelihood that they will come to your show.

Just hanging up flyers and hoping that people will show up is ridiculous. It just doesn't work! No one is going to see a group that they have never heard anything about. This is why you need to tell them about your group, while you give them your flyer. Make friends with them, and convince them to come to your next show. If you do this all the time, at every show and opportunity, you'll start running into the same faces. The more often you run into these people the more interested they will be in seeing your group.

So make flyers, but don't post them on telephone poles or silently hand them to strangers. Instead, make flyers and use them as tools to network with new people. Use them simply as reminders for your current followers and post them on your social networking sites. Used properly, they can affect your group's draw.

Use a Catapult Event to Grow

A catapult event is an event where you position your group so that your band looks bigger than it really is. This is done to generate a buzz and change perceptions. There are three simple but effective types of catapult events: your group's very first performance ever, winning a battle of the bands, and a record release party. Other catapult events may include opening for a national act or showcasing for a record label, but these are reliant on other people and outside of your control for planning purposes.

If you've already been performing live for a while, then it may seem to be too late to utilize your first performance as catapult event. But you can achieve a similar result by taking a long break from live shows and putting together a whole new show, or even by changing your group's name. Frankly, as long as you don't have a record or a decent fan base, then changing your name will not hurt you.

If your group has fallen into the trap of playing too many shows too close together for too long, then you have probably destroyed your chances of developing a strong draw. In this case you should seriously consider a name change. Your first performance can really help set the tone for your group; it's a lot like a first impression on a stranger.

If your first show is packed with cool friends and acquaintances, and you put on an amazing, fun show, people will want to come see you again. They'll keep coming back as long as you don't start playing out all the time and destroy that cool scene. If you're playing live more than once every 6 weeks in your home market, you're making a huge mistake that will eventually destroy your draw, if it hasn't already.

Another great catapult event is a battle of the bands competition. What do you think happens when your group wins a battle of the bands in front of a sold out crowd of people screaming their heads off? Besides the prizes, you'll be making a big impression to a lot of people. And people love to name drop.

How many times has one of your friends told you about how they met some celebrity or know someone that has met some celebrity? In the same vein, whenever the topic of music comes up, they are going to tell everyone they know that their friend's band just won the battle of the bands. They'll go on about how the place was so packed they couldn't move. They will talk about how exciting it was and how they can't wait for your next show. Hopefully, they'll tell everyone they know to come see your band.

That's not all that winning a battle can do for your band; you'll also be able to add this achievement to your press kit and bio. Bios are really just a resume for your band. When an industry person hears that you won a few local competitions, opened for a bunch of national acts, or sold a bunch of records, they will start paying attention. Battles can grow your fan base, help you gain the respect of close friends and fans, and improve your bio dramatically.

I love the battle of the bands. I understand the important psychological nuances that battles can deliver for bands. Winning a battle is a great feat that can help the winning groups with their status in the market, and the prizes are a great reward. The battles are also great vehicles for bands, since they turn a local show into an event. It is a fact that when a local show is an event—like a battle of the bands— the attendance practically doubles. This is why you need to make every single show you schedule some kind of an event.

These are not the only reasons that battles are such powerful tools for bands. One of the most powerful ways to grow your band is by creating a genuine connection with your fans. When your fans are screaming your group's name out after an amazing performance, it creates a bond between you and your fans. I know of no other event that cements a bond as strongly between a band and its fans.

The third, and probably the most effective catapult event of the three, is the record release party. It's the most effective, because it is all about your group. It is also the point at which your band has a record and starts to be taken more seriously by everyone. When you have a record, you establish credibility and position yourself as an up-and-coming group in your market.

A record release party is also one of the easiest events to promote. It's really hard for a friend or follower to tell you they can't come to your record release party, so you should be able to get every single person you know to come to this event. The key is to ask *everyone* to be there. The day after you sell out your record release party, your friends and following will be telling everyone about your group. After the party, all of your friends and followers will be able to play your music for other potential followers. Hopefully, some of them will fall in love with your songs and become true fans.

I can't say this enough: you should make every show an event. Using record release parties or playing annual events (like a Labor Day Cook Out) can help your group grow. You should hold as many of properly-spaced out events as possible, but always be very careful not to over saturate your market.

Networking Daily = Success

When I was in the AKT, Richard and I went out almost nightly, networking everywhere we could. When we booked our first event, we took four months to network it. The first thing we did after we confirmed our date was to look up all the other concerts and events where we wanted to pass out tickets and flyers. We were very aggressive, and in four months, we only missed a few of these events.

We tried to sell tickets wherever we could, and we passed out flyers to everyone we could find.

Each week, we would look through the weekly music magazine and update our calendar with all of the new concert listings. At some concerts, we would get backstage to meet with the artists. I remember one show in particular where we got backstage at a Jane's Addiction concert and I met Perry Farrell. I was a little drunk, and I think I annoyed him when I kept asking why he didn't play "Jane Says." Richard and I didn't really care what people thought of us.

If I'd known what I know now, I would have been a better networker. I would have tried to befriend Perry instead of drunkenly repeating the same annoying question over and over again. At the time, I didn't realize we were networking. I thought we were promoting, and the idea of networking was not on my mind. But remember, that the best way to get a rock star or a record exec to like you is the same as with anyone else: be sincere and genuine. Any time you get the chance to network with someone that's on a level above you, you need to do so as professionally as you can.

Social Networking

The social Internet boom was the biggest thing to happen to local bands in the last decade. Groups can now share their music with strangers and promote their shows for free to thousands of people with the push of a button. A lot of groups out there are misusing the technology by spending all of their time trying to add friends in other countries or in cities where they have never been, and probably will never go. They are not using the tool for its highest and best use, which is networking.

Use your social networking sites to make real friends and new fans by having real conversations with people. Just like you would in real life, you want to look into the people your friending on your site and see what they like to do and what bands they listen to. Find common interests and start a real conversation with them, and then tell them about your group. Everyone in the band needs to get involved in this process. You need to make new friends and get them out to your shows.

Everyone these days is a member of some social network. It is easier to reach producers, record company executives, agents, promoters, and clubs than ever before. You need to start researching record companies, talent agencies, band managers and any other company that can help your group. Find people who are already working with groups you like and respect. Then reach out to them. Contact them via social networking, email or even by phone whenever possible. Let them know what you're doing, send them some music, and ask them what it would take to start a working relationship. Continue to search the internet and find people who can help you.

 Have a weekly band meeting where you discuss all aspect of your band's career.

The 1,000 Person Guest List

Use a guest list to grow awareness and create a buzz about your group. For the first show The AKT played, we created a huge guest list to help produce a buzz around our band, and it was a *tremendous* success. Like I said before, we sold 200 pre-sale tickets to the show, but we also had a 500 person guest list that we used to invite people within the music industry.

If we knew a person, we would sell a ticket to them. If we found a person working in the music business, and did not have a personal relationship with them, then we would tell them about our show, and put them on the guest list. The point is to sell as many tickets as possible, and then give away tickets to anyone who won't buy one. Do everything you can to fill the room and to create a buzz.

As discussed in Chapter Two, we tried to create the biggest guest list we could, including college radio DJs, local writers, music and record store employees, cool people in restaurants or coffee shops, club owners, local promoters, and engineers from local studios. We invited anyone else who had a job in the entertainment or music business. We would also put anyone on the guest list who said they would come, but refused to buy a ticket.

More than over 100 people showed up from the guest list or with a complementary ticket. Anytime you can get a 20% return on a free ticket or guest list of that size, you're doing great. If I knew what I know now, I would have created a guest list of 1,000 people or more. Not only were we able to get an extra 100 people to attend our show, but it helped us create a huge buzz in our home market.

You see, the music business is a small, well-connected world. Everyone within the music business seems to know to everyone else…and they talk. When one club owner or writer finds out about some new group, they talk to everyone else about that group. The writers go to clubs and talk to everyone, club owners talk to ad reps, local DJs talk to people on their request lines, and so on and so on. We were able to get an entire town talking about our group, just by sending personalized invites to every influential person in the local music scene.

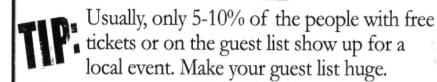

TIP: Usually, only 5-10% of the people with free tickets or on the guest list show up for a local event. Make your guest list huge.

This guest list had a huge local impact. We had the local paper calling us for an interview and every college radio station in town began playing our songs. A very prominent local band manager contacted us, and he promptly started managing our group. All this happened *before* we had even played our first show! Create a huge gust list for every show, but especially your first show or your record release party. Catapult events are the easiest to promote and this will cause your guest list to have the maximum impact.

Amazing Live Shows

Follow the steps in this chapter, plus the advice in Chapter four regarding your shows, and you'll see immediate results regarding the growth of your local fan base. If you continue to improve as musicians, writers, and networkers, you'll be selling out shows sooner that you think. An amazing show is as simple as a handful of goods songs, a well-rehearsed/entertaining set, and a huge crowd of people. If you do it right, fans will beg you for tickets to your next show!

RECAP

- Book your shows at venues that correlate to the size of your fan base.

- Create a scene based around your band to make ticket selling easier.

- Once you can pre-sell tickets to 1/3 of a venue's capacity, you'll have enough draw to not sell pre-sale tickets at every show you play.

- Use fliers to create name recognition and to help you network.

- Catapult Events are great ways to grow your band.

- Network with as many people and as often as possible.

- Use a guest list to grow awareness and create a buzz about your group.

CHAPTER 7

Getting Good Gigs

"Try not to become a man of success,

but rather try to become a man of value."

-Albert Einstein

Clubs Pay Based on Draw

The fact is, most local groups do not understand how or what their pay is based on. Now for the most part, clubs and promoters do not pay groups for their talent or their performance. Frankly, any club or promoter that paid groups based on perceived talent would certainly go out of business.

You see, a club's income does not go up depending on how good any certain group's performance is or how talented they are. A club's income only fluctuates depending on the number of people that attend that particular show or event. Therefore, groups cannot be paid based on the quality of their performance. Instead they are paid according to their draw, which is the number of people that a group can bring to their shows.

It doesn't matter if you're playing a small concert club or a stadium. Either way, you're going to get paid based on the number of people that want to see you play. This is how Radiohead, Killswitch Engage, Dave Mathews, and all unknown local groups get paid when playing a concert venue. Any concert promoter or club that doesn't understand this goes out of business very quickly. This is the biggest reason that clubs and promoters rarely book unknown talent from outside of their own geographical area.

Concert clubs, theaters, and arenas do not have built-in crowds that come every night to see local music. When was the last time you went to a concert club on a whim to see who was playing? Probably never!

Now, there are venues and certain people that do pay groups for talent and not their draw, such as wedding planners. Wedding planners pay groups based on performance alone.

Corner bars also do this, but then you'll usually need to cater to their crowd by playing cover songs or a certain kind of music that their patrons enjoy. Someone holding a special event, a party, or a dance will usually pay a group based solely on the performance, but once again you'll have to cater to his or her crowd. So there are certain situations where groups can be paid based on performance alone. But, if you're playing in a concert venue and you want to be paid, then you're going to need to bring people.

The Numbers Matter

Your group is not going to get paid for the quality of your songs. It just doesn't work that way at the local level. You could write the greatest song ever, and if no one hears that song or buys that song, then you're not going to get paid for that song. It makes no difference whether it's the greatest song ever, or the worst. Your income is only going to be based on the number of units you sell, or the number of times that song gets played on the radio. People must want to hear that song, or be willing to pay to hear it, or you get nothing.

Most artists tell me that they're not in it for the money, which is fine. But understand that the more money you make creating music, the better chance you're going to have of making a career for yourself in this industry. If your group never generates any income, then you'd better be independently wealthy or some kind of trust fund baby. Without sales, labels will not continue making your records, agents are not going to book you, and managers will not be able to continue helping you with your career. If you want a career in music, then making money is a necessary part of the process. Without it how can you afford to continue?

If you're turned off by this reality, then there's nothing wrong with never leaving your basement to play live or bothering to record and release your music. Simply play your songs for yourself in your practice spot. I just want you to understand that if you want the world to hear your songs, then it's going to take money to achieve that goal— both making money, and spending money.

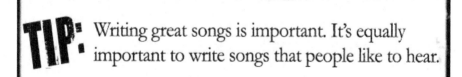

TIP: Writing great songs is important. It's equally important to write songs that people like to hear.

Studios, equipment, agents, managers, and record labels either cost money or expect to make money. We all have to eat, don't we? Without all of these things, people, and companies behind you, your music is never going to reach the masses. Obviously, it's a personal choice to decide how far you want to go, but I'm guessing you take your music career at least somewhat seriously if you're buying a book about the music business. The music business is exactly that: a business. The sooner you embrace that, the further your group is going to go.

If Talent = Sales

Yes, in a perfect world, your group would be paid based on how good your songs were, on how hard you work at practice, and on the quality of your live shows. However, we live in the real world where a group's value is determined by sales and sales alone. Record labels base your pay on sales, not on how many great reviews you get or whether you win a Grammy. Great reviews or winning a Grammy can help you to sell more of your music, but it is not the review or the Grammy that increases your pay—it's what happens as a result of the review or the Grammy.

It's true that labels, agents, and managers look for talented songwriters and performers in the hopes that other people will recognize and embrace their talent and then hopefully buy their music. The more music they sell, the longer their careers can last and the more people they can reach with their music. Remember that the music business is one part music and an equal part business. Start thinking in other people's terms, and you'll get a lot further in the music business and in life.

RECAP

- Concert clubs pay bands based on draw, not on how good they are.

- Concert clubs, theaters, and arenas do not have built-in crowds that come every night to see local music.

- The more money you make creating music, the better chance you're going to have of making music your career.

CHAPTER 8

Gigs in Other Cities

"I'm just taking one step at a time.
I could zigzag one way, but it's not usually on purpose."

-Beck

The Out-of-Town Gig

Every group wants to book out-of-town gigs. It makes them feel like they're going somewhere, like they are reaching out into the world. I have had groups from every city around the country tell me the same thing: "Our local music scene sucks!" Many of these groups think that if they could just play somewhere else, somewhere where people really appreciate music, their group could really make it. They seem to think that their music scene is dead. The only problem with their theory is that they're wrong.

Their music scene is not dead. Frankly, their scene is no different from the scene in the city next to them, or the city after that one. Most major cities around the country are very similar, with similar music scenes. Even if these disenchanted groups were right, and there were all these magical cities where loads of people are going out to see live music, why would these people go to see a group that they have never heard of before? Well they wouldn't! You're not going to get this amazing show in some other city and suddenly get discovered. The only time that really happens is when you are purposely showcasing for labels or VIPs at a festival or on a showcase designed for that purpose.

In reality, you shouldn't even consider playing shows out of town unless your group already has a great following in your own home market. Other reasons to play out-of-town gigs include showcasing for people that can help you with your career, or having some connection in a market that will help ensure that your appearance will be successful. This is the only way it's worthwhile. Playing out of town will usually only help your band if it's some kind of opportunity to meet connected people. Another reason you might want to play out of town is to polish up for an important gig. Then the out-of-town gig can help to prevent overexposure in your hometown.

Getting paid a bunch of money to increase the size of your band fund is also a terrific reason to accept a gig out of town. Now that's not very likely, but it does happen for some groups, especially if they also play covers. Out of town shows are expensive, distracting, and can be disappointing to the point where they can hurt your group internally. There is a place and a time for the out of town gig, but it's not when you're first getting started. Wait until you have built up your following in your hometown to over 200 people, and then you can start thinking about touring.

In The Beginning

In the beginning, you shouldn't even consider playing out of town unless the show falls into one the categories I just discussed: for experience, money, or to build relationships with important people. However, if things are moving forward, then there will come a time when your band will need to start touring. Once your group is doing really well, and you can honestly say that you're one of the biggest groups in town, and you have at least one record to sell and promote, then it's time to start thinking about shows outside your own market.

When you first start touring, your main objectives will be to get better live, to get life experience, and to show the music industry that you are serious about your musical career. You must show them that you're willing to get out there and do it without anyone else's help. It's hard and expensive. You'll need to watch your money by trying to find free places to sleep or by crashing in your van at night. You'll need to shop at grocery stores to save money and eat healthier.

Try to plan these out-of-town undertakings carefully. First, decide where you're going to tour. Pick nearby cities where you have roots, if possible. Pick cities where you know the most people and cities that are close, so you can get some of your local fans to travel out to see you. Once again, your goal will be to develop the strongest draw you can in each market. Try to play with other similar, well-drawing groups. Always build strong relationships with all the bands you play with in each market.

> **TIP:** If you're going to tour, it's a good idea to start out small. Pick nearby cities and head out weekend warrior style. The crowds will be bigger and if something goes wrong, you'll be close to home.

A List of Touring Necessities

1. You must have a decent draw of at least 100 people in your home town—preferably 200 people—before you even consider setting up a tour. Once you have this kind of draw, you should be making at least $300-$1,000 a show and your local relationships within the music industry should be quite strong. This will allow you the capital to venture out and the connections to help you get into certain cities. Most club owners know other club owners from neighboring cities. If you're selling out a club, they should be happy to put in a good word for you with the people they know. Your strong draw also gives you a good base of people that you can invite to your out-of-town shows. Getting your hometown fans out to neighboring cities will help you to create a better atmosphere when you play there.

2. You must have an amazing live show that blows people away. Any time you venture out away from home, you're going to lose what I call your home field advantage. Even if you're able to get as many as 50 local fans out to see you in some other city, it's not going to be enough to fill the room. Therefore, you're going to need to play with other good-drawing groups that also have strong draws, and you're going to need to knock people's socks off to get them out to see you again. Make sure that your live show is amazing and that you impress people—also make sure you connect with them.

3. You must play in the right venues. Just as you must play in the right venues in your hometown, you must also do the same thing in other cities. Make sure you're playing reputable venues that are not too big or too small. Base it on your draw and the draw of the other groups that you're going to play with that night.

4. You are going to need to sell music and merchandise at these shows. It makes no sense to play somewhere, impress everyone, and then leave without giving potential new fans a way to remember you. You must have music, T-shirts, and other items for sale, and you must sell as much merchandise as possible. The more you sell, the better chance you have of getting people back to your next show.

5. You must have your next date in that city confirmed before you hit the stage that night. If you're trying to build a fan base in a new city and you book a date without knowing when you're going to return, then how are you going to reach all these new people again? Make sure you have flyers ready and that you tell all your new fans about your next date in town. Try to make it about 6-8 weeks later and try to make as many friends after the first show as possible. Sell them presale tickets to your next event that night. This helps you to get commitments from people right there and then, helping to ensure a good turn-out for the next time you play there. Use the flyers you created for your next show as a tool to meet new people. Walk up to strangers after the show and ask them what they thought of your band. If they say they liked you, hand them a flyer and ask them to come back for your next show. If they say they will, sell them a ticket on the spot. Get commitments!

6. You must have a way to reach your new fans. Get email addresses, Twitter, MySpace and Facebook URLs, and anything else that can help you reach all the people you meet. After you get their information, send them thank you messages the very next day after the show. Anything that you can remember about the conversation you had with them should be included in your message. The more personal your message feels the better chance you'll have of getting them out to one of your shows. Also, remind them of your return date and ask them again to attend and to bring friends. Create a dialog with as many people as possible, and continue to motivate everyone you can to come to your next show.

RECAP

- Only play out of town shows if your group already has a great following in your own home market.

- When you're ready to start touring, keep in mind that it is an expensive and difficult process. Be smart about with your money and with your health.

- Choose the cities you decide to tour in carefully. Try to play in cities within driving distance or where your band has roots or connections.

STEP 3:
Write Great
SONGS

CHAPTER 9

Where to Start

"You don't know how much artists go through to make it look so easy.
It's all in the practice."

- Lauryn Hill

Where Do Stars Come From?

Most people believe that amazing artists are born with special talents. I once heard Sharon Osbourne say, "You're either born with it or you're not." Now I love Sharon, and she has done an amazing job with Ozzy's career, but in this area, she is dead wrong. Great artists are not born; they are self-made. This is such an important fact that I almost named this book after it. Sure, some people are born with genes that give them certain advantages, but those genes are not the difference between a good and a great artist.

Take a look at the three biggest artists or groups from the 50's, 60's and 80's: Elvis, The Beatles, and Michael Jackson. When I talk about The Beatles, most people immediately conjure up visions of musical genius. When asked, most people assume that the Beatles were born with special talents or musical abilities. But the real story of The

Beatles is very different than you might expect. The Beatles were an average group from Liverpool, England, just outside of London. They were no worse or better than any of the other groups from that area. Then, they got an opportunity to go to Hamburg, Germany, where they played in the Red Light District. This particular gig required that they play seven days a week, ten hours a day, for months at a time. They took on this task several times early in their careers. Their manager has said that The Beatles weren't very special until they got back from Hamburg; after they got back, they were amazing.

What do you know about Elvis Presley? Did you know that he was a perfectionist and a workaholic, and that he would record take after take until he felt that a song was prefect? What do we know about Michael Jackson? His dad had him in dancing shoes almost before he could walk. Michael has said that his rehearsal schedule was so vigorous, he felt like he had lost his childhood. These three artists are considered to be three of the greatest of all time, and their common denominator is the amount of time they dedicated to their art.

The same is true in all areas of life. The more time you spend rehearsing or working on something, the better it gets. So if you're serious about a career in music, then make sure you're putting in the time and the work it takes to get to the top.

What's The Music Business About?

In the winter of 2000, my business partner and I held our first of many music festivals. We would fly in A&R reps from different record companies. At these festivals, the one question I always asked these reps was, "What are you looking for when you sign a new artist?" At some point in every answer, I would hear, "We're looking for great songs." Now think about this for a minute. What are you looking for when you enter a record store or change the station on the radio?

Aren't you also looking for great songs? You don't fall in love with an artist unless you first fall in love with their music, right? Do you walk into a music store (or search iTunes) and look for the album with the coolest cover? No! You look for albums with songs you like.

The music business is about songs! If you're capable of writing great songs, then you'll get noticed; it's really that simple. There are literally thousands and thousands of local groups in almost every major city—they are absolutely everywhere. My company books between 7,000 and 10,000 local groups a year. Unfortunately, most unsigned local groups do not yet have good songs, or any radio-friendly songs. In fact, most local groups have songs that are too long, have too much instrumentation, and don't have a single hook anywhere to be found. If they do have a good hook, they don't bother to repeat it for fear that the song will not be original enough. Go through your iPod or your phone. How many local groups' songs do you have? You probably have very few, if any. Ironically, I believe that if groups worked on the right things at practice, almost every one of them could have good or even great songs.

Do the Right Things

There are over a million unsigned groups in the U.S., and most of them don't have a single decent song. How is that possible? It's really quite simple: most groups are not putting in enough time crafting their art, and most are working on the wrong things at practice. If Kobe Bryant or Michael Jordan went to practice everyday and threw a football around for 70% of the time, how good do you think they would be at shooting hoops?

Here is what the average group will do: they put a group together, write twelve songs in two months, and then they start playing as many shows as they can find. Two years later, they're still playing the same twelve songs they wrote in those first two months. Does this sound familiar to you? Is this what your group does? Obviously, this is a bit of an exaggeration, but honestly not by much. Most groups only have between 10 to 15 songs and spend most of their time rehearsing the same old songs over and over again to get ready for their next show. They spend about 70% of their rehearsal time rehearsing old songs, about 15% discussing group business, and about 15% of the rehearsal time writing new material.

Now consider that the average group rehearses 2-3 times a week for about 2-1/2 hours per rehearsal. If you add this up you get a total of 7-1/2 hours a week. If only 15% of that time is used for writing new material, then the average group only spends about 1 HOUR per week writing new material. This is an average, so if you write for 3 hours one week, but not again for three weeks, then you are averaging about 1 hour per week. How can anyone that spends one hour a week doing anything expect to get good at it? Do you think Michael Jordan would have been a star if we worked on his true craft for one hour a week? Famous author Malcolm Gladwell, writer of "Blink" and "The Outliers," explains that it takes 10,000 hours to become an expert at anything. If his numbers are accurate, then it will take the average unsigned group that only spends one hour a week writing, 192 years to become expert song writers.

In order for your group to get good at writing, you need to spend as much time writing as possible. Start writing all the time, everywhere you can, together and apart. Write, write, and then write some more! Why would you think that you need to rehearse your set into the ground for a show with a crowd of 15 people?

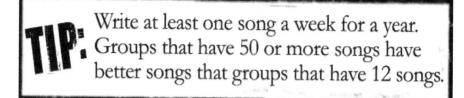

TIP: Write at least one song a week for a year. Groups that have 50 or more songs have better songs that groups that have 12 songs.

Make or Break You

How long are your rehearsals? If the average group spends about 2-1/2 hours together a few times a week how much of that time is wasted? Some of that time ends up being used for set up, group discussions, and rehearsing old material. By the time all that is done, there is not much time left for writing new material or fine tuning material that still needs work. When coaching groups, one of the first things I look at is the length of each rehearsal. I always recommend that groups find ways to increase the length of their rehearsals. If you have a limited amount of time you can commit to your project, it's always better to have longer rehearsals than a bunch of short rehearsals each week.

With longer rehearsals, less time is wasted on set up and group discussions. This makes each rehearsal more effective and productive. More importantly, you give yourselves the opportunity to reach a *higher* writing level while you are working on your material. Have you ever been writing a new song when all of a sudden, it feels like something has come over you? It's as if the song is pouring out of you, almost like it's not even coming from you. This is called a writer's high. When it happens, it's an amazing feeling, and you're able to write some of your best stuff while in this state.

We have all heard stories about some famous group that wrote their best or most successful song in five minutes. It happens all the time and to almost every group in every genre of music. Yes, they wrote their best song in five minutes, but what no one talks about is the fact that they wrote their best song in five minutes *after* being at practice for several hours. Sometimes, a writer's high happens after writing a bunch of other songs, and the momentum propelled them to a heighten state.

Athletes talk about being in the zone. Writers and musicians talk about having a writer's high. What they are talking about is an inspired performance level that gives them an amazing sensation. It is while you're in that state that you'll be able to create your best music or songs. You want to be in that state for as long as possible. The longer your rehearsals, the better your chances are of reaching peak performance levels, which will give you the best opportunity to create great music.

In my coaching sessions, I ask groups to try to think back to their longest rehearsal ever. They are always amazed when they remember the amount of work they accomplished on that day. I hear stories about how they wrote their best song on that day, and how they wrote that song in just a few minutes. So think back. Do you remember your longest rehearsal? What did you get done on that day?

Here is what I recommend to groups that are serious about their musical careers: spend a minimum of three hours or more at each rehearsal, or don't waste your time rehearsing. Then, at least once a week try to have a rehearsal that's a minimum of 6-hours long. Use this rehearsal to work on writing new stuff and fine tuning your current material. Start to focus on what's being accomplished at each rehearsal. Keep a band journal to remind yourselves of your accomplishments, and to plan what you need to work on at your next rehearsal. Obviously, if you can spend even more time writing, then you're going to get better faster. Your songs will keep improving as well. Don't expect to write great songs, if you're not willing to put in the time. It's just not going to happen.

Commitment

During the coaching process, one question helps me determine each group's level of commitment: is your practice schedule set in stone? In other words, are your practices on the same days and at the same times each week? This question can often help a group determine who is committed to the project and who is just in it for a good time.

Groups that do not have a set rehearsal schedule are almost always not as committed as groups that do have set rehearsal schedules. Sometimes, it's just one individual that hinders the group from keeping a regular schedule, but in reality a group should be able to rehearse with or without all of its members. Only rehearsing when every member is available is not an effective way to get things done.

Once you agree to a practice schedule, what you are really doing is making a commitment—a commitment to your art, and to each other. It says on that day, at that time, the most important thing in your life is your music. It sends a message to the other members of your group, to your loved ones, and to the rest of the world that you are serious and committed to this project. That it really means something to you.

If you do not a have a set practice schedule, what you are actually saying to yourself, the other members of your group, and the world is that this isn't important enough for you to schedule time for it. If that's the case, then why bother continuing to participate in the group? Get involved in something you enjoy enough that you can find the time for it. Success requires sacrifice, and you're going to need to decide what writing great music is worth to you.

Set your rehearsal schedule set in stone. Make each session count by making it long enough to get things accomplished, and try to make writing your central focus. Once you have a rehearsal schedule, understand that sometimes things come up, and you'll occasionally need to be flexible. Just make sure it doesn't become a habit, and never cancel a practice just because one person can't make it. You can always write songs without them or have a sectional rehearsal. For example, if your singer can't make it to practice, use the time to work on the rhythm section, or if the drummer can't make it, work on the melody or vocal parts. It's important to schedule sectional rehearsals anyways, so these occasions are a perfect time for them.

If you don't have that problem, and everyone seems to make it to every rehearsal, then you're still going to need to schedule sectional rehearsals as a part of your practice schedule. At least once a month, break rehearsals into sectional rehearsals so you can work on tightening up your sound. You can also write new material as the guitarist or keyboard player, or other members get together on their parts. Sectional rehearsals tighten up your songs and inspire your members. They can also help to keep things fun and interesting.

 Make it a rule: If someone misses practice, they have to make it up later. This way you can be sure that everyone is committed to the group.

The Dual Tape Recorder Method

The dual tape recorder method is one of the best ways to reduce wasted time and improve your group's song writing abilities. Take a dual tape recording device (or a digital recording device with the same capabilities) to each practice and let one side of the recorder run continuously. Stop it whenever you need to reference any part of the tape. Anytime you're in the middle of a new song, and you hear someone write something cool, you can quickly play it back to communicate what it is that you liked. I have been in countless practice situations where someone wrote a really cool part, and by the time I tried to tell them what I liked, it was lost forever. By having a continuous recording of your songwriting session, it will prevent your group from losing cool new ideas and speed up the process of communicating with each other.

The second recorder is to save new ideas and songs for future rehearsals. How many times have you written a killer song only to go back to practice a few days later and find that someone couldn't remember their part? This forces you to start the writing process all over again, and it may never be as good as your original idea. The dual tape recorder technique prevents this problem from happening, and it archives all of your ideas for future use.

RECAP

- Stars are self-made

- The music business is about great songs

- Have a regular practice schedule

- Spend most of your rehearsal time writing songs

- Have longer rehearsals

- Do not cancel practice just because one of the members of the group can't make it

- Use sectional rehearsals to tighten up

- Preparation and good planning cause spontaneity

- Use the dual tape recorder method to save time and great ideas

CHAPTER 10

Writing Attention-Getting Songs

"The bands that wrote the big, heroic rock songs-

I really wanted to make a record like that."

- Sheryl Crow

2 Kinds of Songs

There are two kinds of songs, and in most cases, your group needs both of them. The first type of song is the "hit" song or radio friendly song, and the second kind is called the album cut. When I say "hit" songs and album cuts, most people immediately think that I am referring to good and bad songs. That's not what I mean at all. Every song on your record should be good. "Hit" songs are songs that have short, catchy, repetitive hooks that immediately get stuck in the listener's head. Album cuts have longer, more complicated hooks. You generally need to hear an album cut a few times before you even like it. If an album cut is a great song, it can end up becoming one of the listener's favorite songs for years to come.

I like to say that radio hits are like a big bowl of chocolate. At first, it's delicious. But if it's all you have, repeatedly, it begins to sort of make you sick. On the other hand, an album cut is like a great tasting salad or piece of chicken; you could eat it almost every day and never get tired of it.

Once again, I'm not saying good or bad. They really are as different as chocolate and chicken, and it's important that you know how much of each kind you need on your record. If a group like Radiohead puts out a record with all kinds of "hit" songs on it and nothing else, they would probably lose their fan base. However, an artist like Britney Spears needs mostly hit songs on her record, as her fans are not quite as sophisticated as Radiohead's fans. Sorry, Britney fans.

Everyone thinks that the hair bands from the 80's are made fun of because of their clothes and crazy hair, but if that were true, then we would also make fun of David Bowie, Mötley Crüe, and a ton of other weird looking groups. You see, the reason we make fun of the hair bands from the 80's is because they only put "hit" songs on their records. The hair bands, more than almost any other genre of music, focused hard on "hit" songs, just like the boy bands or teenybopper groups. As a result, we all bought their albums, and ten months later, we were over them. Many of the groups from the 80's, more than any other decade, are still being made fun of to this day.

So, if you have too many radio friendly songs on your record, you become laughing stocks and destroy your chances of longevity. But if you only put album cuts on your record, then it's almost impossible to get noticed. I believe most groups need a good mix of "hits" and album cuts. However, if you're just starting out, then I recommend that you lean towards "hits" since getting your group noticed should be your first goal.

Do You Have A Hit Song?

Here is a technique that will help you determine if you have a potential hit song: ask yourself, who is the worst singer in your band? This is usually an easy question, but if you find yourself in a band where everyone can sing, then you'll need the help of a close friend or family member who is very familiar with your music and is also a bad singer. Once you've found your bad singer, it's time to take the test.

First, have this bad singer sing the hook to the Rolling Stones song "I Can't Get No Satisfaction." This usually takes a little coaxing; no one that thinks they have a bad voice wants to start belting out songs in front of everyone. So assure them that it's important and that they only need to sing a few notes.

I have found that no matter how bad someone sings, they can usually recognize hooks to radio friendly songs. You're not looking for them to sing well—only that they can recognize the hook in the song. Almost every person I have tested can repeat the hook to this song. Once they pass the test, ask them to sing a few notes to whichever song your band agrees is your "radio hit."

You would be amazed by the number of bands that have a member in their own group who not only can't sing even a few notes to their supposed hit, but who can't even remember the words to it. If the drummer or bass player in your own band doesn't know the hook or the words to the chorus in your "hit" song, then it's not a "hit" song! Now that doesn't mean it's not a good song. It might be a great song, or even your best song. But it's just not a radio friendly song.

There are other things to consider when looking for your "hit" songs. First, you must consider the length of each song. If a song is six-minutes long, then it's not your "hit". Radio almost never plays six-minute songs, especially from a new group. Time each song, and make sure every song over four-minutes long is going to be an album cut. If you want to make a six-minute song into a "hit", then you better cut it down to less than four-minutes. Radio stations play shorter, attention-getting songs that can hold their audience's attention just long enough to get them to a commercial break.

Secondly, ask yourself, how long is the intro? If the intro is a minute long, then it's not a radio "hit". The *only people* who tend to enjoy two-minute-long song introductions are the people performing them! For your first radio hit, your intro should be no longer than ten seconds—preferably less than five seconds. Furthermore, if it's a radio hit, then the hook should be near the beginning and at the end of the song to make it more memorable. How many choruses do you have, and how long is the hook in the chorus? If the chorus repeats only once, has twelve words in it, and your drummer doesn't know half of those words, then once again, it's not your hit song. If a song has more verses than choruses, then it's probably not a "hit" song. "Hit" songs are about hooks, and those hooks need to be the most prominent part of the song.

In my early years, I was in a very creative band that got the notion that great songs were entirely about originality. This "creative" band didn't understand the importance of writing hooky songs. In fact, we used to write songs that were complicated and filled with verses and parts that didn't repeat at all. Frankly, we had so many lyrics that I had trouble remembering them all. The only people that liked any of these songs were the members of our band and a few very close friends, who had been exposed to these songs over and over. Recently, I listen to some of these songs and noticed that we had lots of good parts to our songs. However, our songs weren't coherent or well-structured. We certainly didn't have any songs that an unbiased listener could enjoy without being exposed to them over and over. At that time, we wrote songs that we thought were brilliant, and some *parts* of our songs were outstanding, but none our songs had any structure.

This is probably the biggest mistake I see groups making on a regular basis. They play one of their songs, and a few parts have merit, but the song only seems to touch on the best parts of the song briefly. The hooks don't repeat often enough, or the hooks are just too complicated for the listener. If more groups listened more carefully to the songs they are influenced by, they would see that most quality songs are structured very simply and tend to be very repetitive. In fact, the hook is usually driven into the ground. Listen to "I'm Going Down" by Bruce Springsteen carefully and you'll notice that he sings the word "down" almost 100 times in that song. Most of his songs have a strikingly similar structure and are very repetitive. Bruce was once considered by many critics to be the new Bob Dylan. If a singer/songwriter who is compared to Bob Dylan and called "the working man's poet" can repeat the same phase 100 times in the same song and make it sound good, then maybe it's time to simplify your songs a bit.

I found that I have to be careful when discussing radio "hits" and song structure. A lot of artists and musicians get offended when people try to put things in boxes or suggest that a certain formula or song structure will sell records. Please understand that I am not telling anyone what to write or how to write. In my coaching sessions, I refuse to discuss with my clients whether I think a song is good or not. I strongly believe that music is subjective and very personal. What one person likes, another person dislikes. All I am asking is that everyone open their ears and take a close listen to what is really happening around them (on their favorite albums and on the radio).

I didn't make the rules or create song structure. I am just sharing with you what I have observed. Maybe you don't want your music on the radio, and that is perfectly fine. I consider myself to be an artist first and believe that self-expression is one of the most fulfilling experiences in life. However, as an artist, entertaining at least a few people along the way has always been important to me. I assume that entertaining others is important to you as well. Without solid song structure, it's just not possible to entertain people who are not personally involved in your music or your writing process. This means that pretty much every person in the world, outside of your group, will lack interest in your songs that lack good song structure.

> **TIP:** Once you write a song, try to determine whether it's a "hit" song or an album cut. Do not base this decision on taste, but on the distinct differences between hits songs and album cuts.

Throwing Away Hit Songs

Did you know that most groups throw their "hit" songs away? That's right. They write a "hit" song and then throw it out. You see, artists tend to like their album cuts better than their "hit" songs. Remember, radio "hits" are like a big bowl of chocolate; after you play it over and over, you sometimes start to hate it. In fact, the more a band plays a "hit" song, the more they start to dislike it.

Most people believe that radio is capable of killing songs. We've all heard people say that radio killed this song or that song, but the fact is radio doesn't really kill songs. In reality, a radio "hit" is like a suicide bomber or a kamikaze pilot. How many times have you bought an album and never listened to the "hit", or only played the "hit" until you got sick of it? Consider that over the course of many years, you end up listening to the album cuts on that album you love many more times than the "hit" song. You may even end up listen to the album cuts thousands of times more than the "hit" song. The "hit" that radio stopped playing years ago. Similarly, you still skip it every time you listen to the album.

So, did radio really kill that "hit" song if you've heard the other songs thousands of times more than the radio song? No. The song, by its own nature, had a short life span. It was a big bowl of chocolate, a suicide bomber. It went 100 miles an hour until it ran out of gas. So, as an artist, we hear and play our songs so many times that we start to think that our radio songs suck! Truth be told, they're not necessarily bad songs. We're just sick of them. Their repetitive, uncomplicated hooks are great for radio, because they grab the listener's attention quickly. Unfortunately, these songs also tend to drive us (the artists) crazy after a while.

In 2010, I was speaking at one of our music festivals. When I started discussing how bands tend to throw their "hits" songs away, a group stood up and told their story. They were lucky enough to have gotten some airplay on a local radio station in town. They said that when I started talking about "hit" songs and how artists tend to throw them away, they were shocked. The same thing almost happened to them. The song that the radio was playing was a song they almost threw away. They grew sick of the song and *thought* it sucked, yet all their fans loved it, and now it was getting played on the radio!

Ironically, when I'm coaching bands, I find that their friends and family will know which song or songs are the radio-friendly songs and the band will not. Your group can do a lot of things, but one thing you should never do, without help is deciding which of your songs have "hit" potential. If you want to know which of your songs is your "hit", ask your best friend, your girlfriend, or the fan that has seen your and heard your group the most. When you're planning to release a record, one of the best things you can do is ask your fans which songs they like the most. Trust their judgment over your own. Most of the time, a band's fans will have a better perspective on their songs than the members of the group.

Not long ago, we began managing a group, and we realized that one member's mom knew better than the group as to which songs were better for radio. They were sick of their radio hit and she wasn't. I knew before I even heard any of their songs, that she was right, and the band was wrong. They thought that a different song was their radio hit, but it was definitely an album cut. It was, in my opinion, a much better song, but it wasn't a radio hit. Please find a way to get it out of your head: good does not mean radio "hit". If the song doesn't follow the structure that radio stations have been playing for over 50 years, then radio isn't going to play it. There are radio songs or "hit" songs, and there are album cuts. Radio songs get people's attention, and album cuts keep people interested. Make sure you have both of them on your record.

Writing is a Learned Skill

Writing is a learned skill; the more you write, the better you get at it. Lots of groups spend most of their time practicing the same ten or twelve songs they wrote two years ago instead of writing new songs. In life, we get better at the things we work on consistently. If you want to be a successful recording artist, then you need to spend most of your time learning to be a better writer, or else you need to hire someone to write your material for you.

One of the best ways to learn anything is to study other successful people's styles and works. If you were taking a creative writing class at school, one of the first things they would have you do, would be to examine other great works. Yet in the music business, musicians rarely examine other great songwriters or their work. They tend to just kind of do their own thing. When was the last time you took a close look at another popular artist's work? I believe that it's imperative that you examine the music of people who you respect. I'm guessing that you've probably never really studied any other band's or musician's work. If you have, then bravo to you; if you haven't, then start examining what other artists are doing. Time their songs, count the words in their choruses, and count how many times the chorus repeats. Figure out how long each part is and how many parts are in a particular song. Determine what it is that you like about their work, and why it's popular (if it is popular). I know that some people are going to read this and get really turned off and start talking about originality. In every other artistic field, like painting for example, it's not only accepted to study other artists, but it's expected. Why is this frowned upon in the music world?

If you were taking a course on writing, your teacher would also have you write a lot, but in lots of different areas. He wouldn't just have you write in one particular field. He would assign different kinds of writing to give you more experience and to help you build a strong foundation. Heck, the school would even make you take classes that have nothing to do with writing to give you a well-rounded education. That education would provide you with more life experience and it would end up giving you more to write about.

You might only like hard rock or metal, but finding influences outside your circle of experience will help you to dramatically improve your writing skills and give you a hand in creating new writing opportunities.

Learn to listen to music from an observational viewpoint, and not just as a passive listener.

Your Sound

You must know who and what your band sounds like, if you want to make it in the music business. If you ask the average local group who they sound like, most of them can't give you an answer. Even the ones that do will often take fifteen minutes to explain their sound. The most popular answer is, "We are completely original. We don't sound like anyone else." This is usually said with pride and a sense of accomplishment.

Somewhere along the way, someone got the idea that record companies and music fans are looking for something completely different. It's simply not true. We're all just looking for something that we enjoy. If your group is really completely different from any other band, then no one is going to touch you with a ten foot pole, not labels and certainly not listeners. A sound that's too original is usually classified as avant-garde, and very few people have the patience for that kind of experience. The funny thing is that the groups that claim to be completely original rarely are, and claiming to be only hurts them.

When someone asks you what your group sounds like, and you tell them, "no one," they are going to get bored or turned off. The easiest and more effective way to describe your music is to compare it to something people can relate to. "We are completely original," or "I can't explain our sound," might seem cool to you, but it's not to anyone else. Maybe you can't explain your sound, but that's a boring answer to the listener. How excited would you be if you asked

someone what you thought was a simple question and then got a five
minute explanation that didn't come close to answering your question?
Have you ever sat in a classroom where the teacher started poorly
explaining something that you didn't understand? I'll bet you either got
frustrated or bored stiff. Does that really seem like a good way to
impress a new potential fan?

The next most popular answer in my experience is, "We sound
like Dave Mathews," or "We sound like Tool." These kinds of answers
are also bad. They're boring and they lose the listeners interest, because
everyone already knows what Dave Mathews sounds like. That answer
provides no mystery or uniqueness. You also have no idea whether or
not that person likes Dave Mathews. If they do like Dave Mathews,
they might not be drawn to your group, because there's already a Dave
Mathews, and in their mind, he probably does Dave Mathews better
than you. If they don't like Dave Mathews, you lose as well. Why
would they be interested in a group that sounds like something they
already know they don't like? Instead, you need an interesting, truthful
answer. Check out this demonstration:

If you had a choice between listening to only one group of the
following three examples, which one would you choose?

1. "We're completely original. I really can't describe our sound,
   because we don't sound like anybody else out there. You just
   kind of have to hear it for yourself."
2. "We sound exactly like Dave Mathews."
3. "We're a cross between Metallica and Madonna. Our lead
   guitarist, who only has three fingers, plays a distorted banjo that
   he lights on fire at the end of our set."

Now you might not like Metallica or Madonna, but I'll bet you want to
know what that sounds like. You have to know how to describe your
group in a fast, interesting way. Do not tell people that your band is

completely original. Instead explain your group's sound and your group's shows in a completely original way. In a way that will get people interested in seeing and hearing your band.

Since the most effective way to grow your band is by networking, you must be able to grab people's interest so they want to buy your music or come to your shows. Here's the most important part of this story. If you were in a band that was a cross between Metallica and Madonna you would be the next big thing.

Instead of listening and getting influenced only by the music that you like or what's most popular today, you need to start listening to things outside your comfort zone. You need to start stretching as a person and learning about all kinds of music. In return, your music will get more interesting. Here are some other examples of attention-grabbing descriptions of bands:

- "We're like Johnny Cash, except we play some of the hardest metal music you've ever heard, and in our band, Johnny's the coolest chick in Chicago. Our singer is out of her mind, but in a super cool way."
- "We sound like Tori Amos meets David Bowie, but without the piano. Our guitarist sometimes plays a de-tuned upside violin and our drummer plays on a two piece drum kit, but somehow he makes it sound like a ten-piece set.

You want your answer to be as interesting as possible without being dishonest. Start to really listen to your music and figure out who and what you sound like, and figure out where you can take that sound.

Find other ways to write new material. If you're using only one style to write, then you need to add several other methods. For instance, if your group only writes as a unit in a jam-style manner, then have each member write new material on their own. Then present it to the group so they can help rewrite it or improve it. On the other hand, if all the members write on their own and never as a group, then try writing as a group. One of the best examples of a group using new writing methods is the story of how The Beatles wrote The Sgt. Pepper's album. They approached writing this record as fictional characters, alter-egos. Each member took on their own fictional character and wrote from that person's perspective rather than their own. To this day, it's still considered one of the greatest records of all time. So find as many ways to write as you possibly can and write as often as possible. You'll grow as writers, and as people.

RECAP

- There are 2 kinds of songs that all bands need: "hit songs" and album cuts.

- Most groups throw their radio hits away.

- Writing is a learned skill. The more you write, the better you get at it.

- Describe your group in a fast, interesting way to grab the interest of prospective fans.

STEP 4: Make GENUINE CONNECTIONS with Your Fans

T-Shirts are Powerful

"A T-shirt can do more for your group
than a billboard in a high traffic area."

- John Michalak

Use T-shirts to Grow

Groups constantly ask me what I think are the best ways to promote their group. By now, if you've been following along, you've probably realized that I don't believe you can promote an unknown local group. I believe the only way to grow a local group's following is for the group to network, which is why T-shirts are so important for local groups. As a local group, you need to buy and sell as many T-shirts as possible. Use every opportunity you have to sell them. A T-shirt is a walking, talking billboard—with the emphasis on *talking*.

Now, a billboard is great promotional tool for anyone that is selling a product that is widely known in the marketplace. For an unknown artist, a billboard on some crowded highway would be completely ineffective in helping them connect with a new audience.

In fact, it would be more useful as a publicity stunt than a promotional tool, if there was some way a local group could afford to advertise in that manner.

Lots of cars will drive by and see the billboard, but it would be forgotten quickly. It might build a mild level of name recognition, but it won't generate any record sales or sell any tickets to their shows.

How could it possibly help? Of coarse it can't. The people who drive by would have no idea what that group's music sounded like, and they probably wouldn't even realize what it was advertising. How could they? Music is subjective, intangible and difficult to describe in words, even with a picture and a snappy tag line.

When a billboard is used to promote an artist or an upcoming tour, it is for a group that everyone probably knows, so the billboard doesn't need to describe that group's music because consumers are already familiar with it. All that a billboard does is make everyone aware of a *known* artist's upcoming tour or new record release. It cannot do the same for a group that no one has ever heard of before. A billboard will fail in promoting your band, just as an ad in the paper would fail, or any other advertising campaign that uses pictures or words to promote a product. Any advertising campaign that does not have the ability to showcase a group's music repeatedly will be ineffective.

A T-shirt is a completely different story altogether. It's like a mini billboard, except it can *talk*. Well, it can't technically talk, but the person wearing it can! And, if they made the effort to buy your band's shirt and wear it, then they are also likely to speak highly of your group.

If, through some technological miracle, a billboard had the ability to tell every passerby what your band was about and that your band was awesome, then that billboard would be a huge promotional tool.

People are curious by nature. I would be willing to bet that most people checking out a billboard with an unfamiliar band on it would ask, "What the heck is that about?" Well, that's exactly what happens when your fans start buying your T-shirts and wearing them around town. They become walking, talking, word-spreading billboards. The more talking billboards your group has that can tell people about your band, the better. In my first successful local group, we sold over 100 T-shirts before we ever played a show. If you haven't sold at least 100 T-shirts by now, then get on it right away, because word of mouth isn't the only reason T-shirts are so important.

Use T-shirts to Connect

In addition to T-shirts being a great marketing tool, they are also one of the best ways to strengthen your bond with your fans. Once a fan buys something from you, especially a T-shirt or hat that they can wear, they are going to be even more likely to come to all your shows—as long as you're not over-playing in the market, that is. You see, when a fan makes a financial commitment to your group by buying something from you, it does a few things. It's a constant reminder of your group, helping to keep your group in the forefront of their minds. It also helps deepen their relationship with your group. This action sends messages to their subconscious minds: "If I bought this T-shirt, then I must really like this group."

Each sale strengthens your bond with fans who buy something from you. It also gives your fans the opportunity to make new friends every time someone asks about their T-shirt. Being an insider, or an early fan, makes them feel important. Everyone wants to be one of the first fans of a group that becomes huge! If you can make someone feel important, they will love you forever. Buying a T-shirt gets people to like your group more than they already do and gives them an opportunity to tell other people about your group. You can also make a lot of money doing it. If you're serious about your musical careers, then you need to start making money making music.

> Every time you run out of a shirt design discontinue it, at least temporarily. Have the next design ready to go so you can sell more designs to the same people and create demand for old designs.

Use T-shirts to Raise Capital

There are a several ways for your group to generate income immediately. Usually, the first and easiest way is by selling your group's merchandise. I have groups preach to me that they are not playing music for the money. They insist that they should not have to sell tickets or T-shirts. They go on to say things like, "Anything that looks like commerce or business is an abomination and a detriment to the arts."

I never impose my beliefs on others. I just try to share my life experiences with others in the hopes that I may be able to help someone. Frankly, I'm an artist myself, and at some level I wish we lived in a world where these kinds of ideals were realistic. The truth is, at some point in your quest to turn music into a career, you are going to have to come to the realization that sales of music and merchandise is acknowledgement that you've made a connection with fans. If you refuse to generate income because of unrealistic ideals, then your ideals are going to prevent you from doing the very thing you claim to love.

Now, if you're serious about your music, and you are hoping to make a *career* out of it, then you are going to need to generate money. You'll need to make money for yourself, so you can eat and live, and for other... If you want anyone to help you with your career, they need to eat, too. You must start thinking of your group as a business and not just a group. If you have dreams of getting a record deal or selling millions of records, or even just enough records to make a decent living, then you need to run your group like a business. Record companies are not signing groups anymore; they are signing small businesses that have proven track records and good business sense. Yes, the music business is about great songs and talented performers. But these days, labels also want groups to *prove* that they have great songs by generating interest from fans. This means sales and income. It's a very competitive world out there, and if you're going to make it in the music business, then you better start thinking in terms of running your group like a business. Don't worry. It's a very creative business, and coming up with networking ideas, cool merchandise and unique strategies can be really fun and fulfilling.

 TIP: Sell other products, like hats or under garments. Sell anything that you can get your fans to buy.

Doing T-Shirts Right

There are a few other things that you will need to know about T-shirts. First off, start small. Buy inexpensive products that you can mark up 100% and still sell at an affordable price to your fans. I recommend that you try to get shirts for about $4-5 each and then sell them for about $10. Most of your followers are not true fans yet. They are mostly friends and acquaintances, so it's important to make your products as affordable as possible without lessening your group's perceived value.

Do not get fancy, top-of-the-line shirts with a 4-color design on both sides that end up costing you $18 each. You would have to sell those shirts to friends and family members for at least $25 apiece. First of all, that's a not a big enough markup. Any person in business would tell you that you need a bigger margin to cover your miscellaneous costs and any lost or unsold shirts. It's also priced way too high for you to successfully sell to your fans. It's better to sell a hundred $10 shirts quickly, rather than struggle to sell a fewer number of over-priced shirts. Sell all of your affordable shirts, then move on to the next design and do it again. Sell as many shirts and designs as you can, continually making a profit and building a stronger bond between your group and your fans while raising as much capital as possible.

Make sure that you know the right sizes you'll need and estimate what colors and designs your fans would like most. If your fan base tends to wear all black, then don't buy 100 baby blue T-shirts with flowered designs all over them! Get what you think they will buy, not what floats your boat. Obviously, you should stay within the integrity of your group's musical genre. A great way to make sure you get the right sizes (and cover the printing costs), is to sell pre-orders to fans and friends. All you need to do is show a photo of the design to your fans and give them an order form. Collect the money on the spot! Work hard to sell at least half of your T-shirts in advance, so the pre-sales will cover the full cost of the order. Whatever you do and however you do it, start selling T-shirts right now.

RECAP

- As a local group, you need to buy and sell as many T-shirts as possible at every opportunity you have to sell them; a T-shirt is a walking, talking billboard.

- T-shirts are one of the best ways to strengthen your bond with your fans.

- Buy inexpensive products that you can mark up 100% and still sell at an affordable price to your fans.

CHAPTER 12

The Studio

"My friend has a baby. I'm recording all the noises he makes
so later I can ask him what he meant."

-Steven Wright

Preparing for the Studio

Unless you're recording in your own studio or somewhere
that's free and without time limitations, then you're going to want to
properly prepare for this process. The right amount of preparation will
result in time saved, which as we all know is also money saved. Even if
you're not being charged to record, the better prepared you are for the
studio, the better your sessions are going turn out. The better your
sessions, the better your songs are going to sound. Most studio owners
and engineers will tell you that the three biggest problem areas for
groups entering the studio are the following: not knowing their songs
well enough, poor timing, and bad vocal performances.

Ask yourself, do you really know your material? Yes, you know
your parts and you probably know them well, but do you know what

everyone else is doing or playing? I have seen groups that think they know their songs inside and out, but when you ask them what the other members are playing or even what the singer is singing, they usually have no clue. I have then witnessed groups say things like, "That's what you're playing? That's awful!" Sometime a studio session is the first time everyone really hears what the other members are playing, and that's a problem in itself.

In order to avoid this problem, it's a good idea to break off into sectional rehearsals, just like an orchestra might. Rehearse with one member at a time, while the other members do the same thing. This will help you to learn what everyone else is playing and it will help you to make sure that it all sounds good together. Your guitarist doesn't have to know the bass player's parts, but he should at least know what the bassist is playing and why he is playing it the way he is. Is the bass player playing a certain part because it makes the song better, or because it's a hard part to play and that makes him feel good about his ability to play his instrument? Or is he playing this part because he couldn't think of anything better? Start asking good questions; start listening to each other's parts to make sure that they make sense together and to make sure that they enhance each song.

This will also remove some of the musical cues that you might have been relying on during your live performances. A lot of times, players know when to change to the next part because the singer sings a certain word or the guitarist plays a certain chord. In the studio, you might not have these luxuries, especially if the engineer doesn't lay down a dummy vocal track or you can't hear the guitar. So it's important that you learn your parts without the help of these musical cues. Removing these musical cues while preparing for the studio will also help you once you return to the stage. The confidence you will gain will make for a stronger, more relaxed performance, which translates well in a live setting.

Use a Click Track

The best way to improve your timing is to start playing to a click track weeks or even months before you enter the studio. Being in a studio, especially for a new group, is an exciting process which is both fun and stressful. The adrenalin rush can cause confusion or sometimes result in groups speeding up the tempos of their songs. If you had been practicing to a click track for a while, then you'll know exactly how fast you have been playing something. You don't want to get into an expensive studio and start arguing about tempos or song structures. Learning to play to a click track can be a very hard thing for some people. Your drummer in particular needs to be practicing with a click track; not just at rehearsal, but also on his own. Hopefully, he or she has been doing so for years, and you'll be leaps and bounds ahead of the game. If not, he or she needs to start right now, since the drummer is responsible for controlling the tempo of most songs.

TIP: After you write a new song, practice it to a click track. Once you have the right tempo and the number of beats per minute, keep it for your records. This information will be useful when you go to record it.

Take Vocal Lessons

In most groups, you can usually find at least one or two members that have had some kind of formal or informal training, either lessons or schooling. At the very least, usually someone has read a few things about their instrument in a magazine or book, or they have learned a few chords from a friend or another band mate. But most singers on the other hand seem to think that all it takes is for them is to open their mouths and what comes out is music.

Finding a singer that has any formal training whatsoever can be challenging. I could ask 100 groups and I would be lucky to find a hand full of formally trained singers. Mastering your vocal chords is the one of the most difficult things to master. If I were to ask most guitar players to play me a G chord or to hit an A on their guitar, most could without much effort. If I were to ask most vocalists to sing an A note, he or she wouldn't have a clue where to start. Furthermore, vocalists at the local level are not able to hit their notes properly, and frankly most of them are not even aware of the fact that they are off key. They don't usually find out that they're off key until they get into a studio and the engineer tells them they are flat or sharp.

This can cause the whole band to start questioning the singer's ability, and then as the singer starts to feel bad about his or her singing capabilities, things get worse. None of this is necessary; just get some formal training. Yes, it's hard and it takes time, but if you're serious about your career, then it can be done. Most people can learn to sing with the right training and lots of effort. So if your singer has no formal training, then please do not be surprised when you get in the studio with a decent engineer and find out that vocalist is having trouble hitting some of the notes.

Most musicians don't like hearing this, but if you're hoping to be a mainstream artist someday, then your vocalist is the most important aspect of your music. Therefore he or she really needs to be amazing. Professional training can help your vocalist improve his or her singing abilities and it will help improve your group's sound. Even more importantly, singing is hard, and if you're not taking care of your voice or you're not sure how to properly sing, you could lose your ability to sing altogether.

The first thing most singers need to learn is to sing from their diaphragm. If, when you sing, your shoulders go up then you're probably singing incorrectly. Take very deep breathes in-between notes and make sure that your voice is coming from your stomach area. It should look like your stomach is going in and out almost in an exaggerated manner, like when you were young and your Dad or crazy uncle would push his stomach out really far to convince you he was pregnant.

Hitting the Notes Is Not Enough

After your singer gets a good handle on hitting all the notes, then you're going to need to work on his or her sound. It's not enough to just hit the notes; he or she needs to make those notes sound amazing. Tonality is the difference between a boring singer and a breathtaking one. Take Joe Cocker, Janis Joplin, or Bob Dylan. Their tonalities and vocal sounds are half the reason that they became stars. It was the vocal quality, the roughness, and unique vocal sound that drew millions of people to their music. Your singer's voice must be easily recognizable in order to give your group the best chance of achieving success.

What do Cindy Lauper, Bono Vox, and Ozzie Osbourne all have in common? They all have unique voices—the kind of voices that the second you hear *one note*, you already know who is singing. You need to create the same result for your group. Again, make sure your singer is not just working on hitting the notes, but also on the tonality of those notes. Take Tori Amos for example. If you listen to her vocal tracks carefully, you will notice that her singing is very breathy. You can hear her take deep-rooted breathes in-between notes to the point where I question whether they turned up the vocal tracks intentionally during those breathes. For some singers, it's the way they sing their notes; for others, it's their timing or the sound of their voice. It doesn't matter how you achieve this distinctive vocal quality as long as it is effective in making your group sound unique.

Practice getting different sound from your vocal cords. Record these different sounds and start to define a vocal direction for you and your group.

Record Everything

Before you go into any professional studio, pre-record every song you plan to record there. This is process is called pre-production and it's particularly helpful in producing great results for your sessions. This might sound like extra work since that's what you plan to do when you get into the studio, but it will help you in the production of your recordings. The way a song sounds to you when you're in the moment—performing that song live—is a lot different than the way it sounds when you're listening back to it, after it has been recorded.

The more you can duplicate the process you're going to use in the studio to record your songs, the better. If all you have is a single deck tape recorder, then that will have to do. Just record your songs live in your garage or wherever you practice. Now, this will do a few things for you. First, it will provide you a recorded version of each song so you can listen more carefully to your songs. Make sure that you're looking for areas to improve and listen carefully so you can understand each song as a whole unit and not just for its parts. Then after you have your songs recorded, each member can practice their own parts from home more effectively. They can practice each song in its entirety or just the parts in need of work, without wasting everyone else's time. This one step in itself can improve your group performance in the studio probably more than anything else. It allows you and your group to hear each song from a listener's point of view, and it gives each member an amazing tool to help them prepare for the studio independently of each other.

Record for Free

I met and joined my first serious group after I answered an ad in the paper advertising free studio time. As it turned out, it wasn't exactly free studio time, but rather a trade situation, which was fine with me. I would go in and work around the studio for about 20 hours a week in exchange for studio time. They had me cleaning toilets, painting walls, vacuuming, and everything else under the sun. I wasn't even in a band at the time, but thought that compiling a bunch of studio time would help me to find a band and help that band to get off to a great start—and I was right. I wasn't the only person that saw the value in trading their personal time for studio time. Three guys from a group called Serious Nature also answered that ad and within a few weeks of meeting them, I auditioned for their group. Then when we all put the studio time that we had earned together, it was quite a bit of time. We were able to record a full-length album; unfortunately for me, by the time it was ready to be released, I had already joined another group and they ended up replacing most of my tracks.

Getting credit would have been really cool, but the greater value for me at that time was the life experience I gained by working in a studio environment for over a year and recording music there for hundreds of hours by the age of 20. I took that experience with me and repeated the same process in a studio where Trent Reznor of Nine Inch Nails worked. Richard Patrick, my band mate, knew Trent, and Richard was able to get us a discount on studio time. We did pay a little bit of money, but once again, I got great value. This was just before Trent was famous, and he was just about done with his first record, "Pretty Hate Machine." Not only did we get to learn from Trent while we were there, but we got to hear some of "Pretty Hate Machine" before it was release.

I also learned some of the things he was doing at that time. For instance, I found out that Trent had about 10-12 versions of every song that went on that record. He just kept tweaking the record and each song individually until it was prefect. That was a different style of writing than I was used to and it was both interesting and educational. It made me realize that there are many different ways to write. I also learned that he hadn't paid to record his record. Instead, he had been working for little to no pay in exchange for free studio time. It was only my second studio experience, I was already starting to realize that trade was very common in the recording industry.

TIP: Many studios are willing to trade studio time for almost anything of value. Call studios in your area until you find one that is willing to trade studio time for your labor.

From that session forward, most of my studio experiences involved some kind of trade to reduce the cost of the studio time or to get free studio time. In fact, our production company, Gorilla Music, has over 50 deals with studios all over the country, all involving reduced rates for studio time. I have never added it up, but over the years I have probably negotiated deals with over 200 studios, and only a handful of them were unwilling to trade their time. You see, studio time has an expiration date. Any studio that has holes in their schedule would be foolish not to try to get something for that unsold time. Once that time is gone, they can never get it back, which is one of the reasons that the cost of studio time is so negotiable.

The moral of the story is that you don't have to pay full price for studio time. It's usually very negotiable and tends to be based on the number of hours you plan to buy and the time of day or night when you're going to record. Your flexibility can help you to negotiate a better rate. If you're able to record in their off-peak hours or days, then the price will go down. If you're willing to record when their schedule is slow, then you might also be able to negotiate a better deal. All you have to do is ask. First, tell them your situation, that you have a limited budget and that you would love to record in their studio, but that you can't afford their hourly rate. Then ask them if they would be willing to give you a discount to record around their schedule.

In one case, I had my whole band working every weekend and sometimes weeknights painting, landscaping, fixing things, and cleaning out the studio owner's rental properties in exchange for studio time. I would even give this guy's dog a bath about once a week. We would each get $10 an hour for our time, and he was charging us about $40 an hour for his studio time, all of which we negotiated in advance. For each hour all four of us were there, we would get one hour of studio time. After sixteen-hour weekends and another ten hours of work during the week for around six months, we had accumulated a tremendous amount of studio time. The studio owner didn't mind since his staff was on salary and we had agreed to work around his schedule.

It worked out great for everyone involved. The studio owner was able to get lots of work on his properties done for close to nothing, and the engineers were kept busy, helping improving their job security. We were able to spend a lot of time in the studio recording, learning, and gaining lots of experience while we recorded our music.

Finance Studio Time

Later on, I found other ways to get "free" studio time that didn't involve manual labor. Once again, it is not really "free," but it's free enough. Instead of spending hours working on fixing stuff and painting walls, I approached a studio that I wanted to use with the idea of financing their studio time. First, we negotiated the hourly rate, which was based on using their studio around their schedule. This meant that they could bump my sessions if they ended up selling those hours to cash-paying customers, which, keep in mind, was not in their best interest; even with a deal like ours, where we were financing our time instead of paying up front, we were still spending money so the studio wanted to keep us happy as well. They only pushed our sessions if they absolutely had to move them.

Then, we discussed the amount of time they were willing to finance, which was based on our ability to pay them back. We agreed to pay them back with money we planned to make on a record release party. We projected that we would make about $500-$700 from tickets sales, and sell around 100 CD's for another $700, so we felt that we could afford to finance about $1,500 to $2,000 worth of studio time. After coming to these terms, we gave the studio $500 as a down payment—money we raised from selling T-shirts. Then, we financed the remainder of a 50-hour block of time, in which they charged $40 an hour. So we bought 50 hours of time for $40 and hour, which was a total of $2,000. After the $500 down-payment, we still owed them $1,500, which we felt would be easy to make on a properly coordinated and promoted record release party. We signed the contracts and went to work on our pre-production efforts. If you're curious about these kinds of contracts with recording studios, we have an example of this on our website, **www.gorillamusic.com** that can be downloaded and used for your own purposes.

We now work with a group out of New Jersey called Spinn. They were able to pay for their whole record when they signed up on a site called Kickstarter.com. It's a website where people help fund creative projects. Three of the members of the band are waitresses in a local restaurant where they live; within a few weeks, the customers from the restaurant where they work helped them to raise the money they needed. After each donation, they would thank each customer personally through Facebook. The more people they thanked, the faster the donations rolled in for them.

A Home Studio is a Must

When Richard Patrick and I joined forces and starting working on music together, one of the first things we did was to buy some home studio equipment. This was the biggest reason we were able to write better songs than any group I had ever been in before. Writing and playing songs live in your basement while you jam or writing on your own is great, but being able to write and then record what you have written has great benefits. It's one of the best ways to write and to review your work. As I stated earlier, it helps give you a better perspective on what you've written and the opportunity to easily improve areas that need work.

We bought an eight-track recorder and would record the drums on several tracks, then bounce them down to one or two tracks. Then, we would record the guitars, bass, and keyboard tracks, leaving us a few tracks for vocal and backing vocal tracks. Then we would mix them down to cassette and make copies for each of us to review. Later, we would get together and discuss each recording. If we felt we could improve the song, we would rerecord the tracks that we felt needed improvement. We would repeat this process until we were happy with each song. This process helped us to improve considerably as songwriters. If you're serious about having a career in the music business, you need to be able to record your work in order to review and improve your songs, your writing skills, and your understanding of the recording process.

Trading for Musical Equipment

Now back in my days of trading labor for studio time, I got to thinking, why not try the same thing with musical equipment? So I went around to a few music stores in town and asked if they needed any work done around their store. Having a background in home improvement and painting was helpful in finding these opportunities. I was able to find a store that was interested in having their store painted, so I proposed a fee that would be paid to me in trade. Instead of charging them $1,500 in cash, I accepted $1,500 in musical equipment. It worked out great; I needed more equipment and didn't have $1,500 lying around. For the store owner, it was a great way to get his store fixed up without reaching into his pocket. He was able to move his inventory, make a sale, and get his store looking great.

Avoidable Problems

Cheap guitars with bad intonation or old strings, bad sounding amplifiers, poorly tuned drums, and untrained vocalists cause problems and stop progress in the studio. These are a few of the most common things that, with the proper preparation, can be avoided before you enter any studio. Ask any engineer how much time they spend on preventable problems before they even start recording a single note and you'll be very surprised by their answer. If you've never been in a professional studio, then ask a lot of question before you get there. Send the engineer a detailed list of all the equipment you plan to use in the studio and consider the condition of each piece of equipment you plan to use.

After you get the ok from your engineer and he says your equipment is at least adequate to use in his studio, and then take your guitars to a respected music store in the area. Ask them to check each instruments intonation and to give them a quick tune up, so to speak. Replace all the strings on all the guitars, including the bass guitar, a day or two before the sessions—never the day of, or you're going to have tuning issues. Also make sure that you string your guitars properly. Yes, there is a proper way to string guitars, and if you're not sure how, then make sure you learn while you're at your local music store. Make sure you bring extra strings, drum heads, batteries, drum petals, and anything else that could break or need to be replaced when you go into the studio. If you make a list of all the things that have broken or needed replacing before and bring those items with you, that should cover you.

> **TIP:** Make a list of at least 5 studios where you would like to record. Then visualize you and your group recording at each one.

Working in a Recording Studio

I have always said that my dream local group would have great musicians, great songwriters, and would include members that all work in different areas of the music business. One member would work in a recording studio so we could get great deals on studio time. One member would work for the most prominent concert club in town so we could get the best shows and so we would have the inside scoop on everything that's happening in town. Another member would work for a music store, so we could get all the best equipment at the best prices.

And one member would write for an entertainment paper or magazine, so we could hopefully get good press and make great connections.

But if I could only have one member of this dream team, I would choose someone that works in a recording studio. Working in a studio can not only help you to get your group recorded, but it also can teach you so much about the recording process and about songwriting in general. Getting to watch how other people work is one of the best ways to learn new techniques and processes. I highly recommend that at least one person from your group, if not more, find an internship in one or a few of the studios in town and that you try to work out a trade for studio time. This way, you can learn while you earn studio time—a much needed commodity for any local group.

Mix Up Where You Record

It is not unusual for artists to find a studio where they are comfortable, and then for them to use that studio for all their sessions. I understand this logic and once your group is making gold records or winning Grammys, then I will support your decision to do so. However, early in your career, the recording process is as much a learning experience as it is a process to record your material. I always recommend to bands that they try to record in as many studios and work with as many engineers and producers as possible. Working with lots of different people will give you lots of ideas on how to get what you want out of your studio sessions and what you want for your music.

RECAP

- Be as prepared as possible before entering the studio; every member of your band should know every, single song, inside and out.

- Studio time is usually very negotiable and tends to be based on the number of hours you plan to buy and the time of day or night when you're going to record.

- There are a number of ways to avoid paying out of pocket to record in a studio, like trading goods or your time for recording time or by working out a financing deal with the studio.

- Learn as much as you can about what happens in a recording studio; the more knowledge you're able to retain about the recording process, the easier it's going to be on both you and the engineers in the studio.

Selling Your Music

"With all my fans, I got a family again."

-Tupac Shakur

True Fans

Many local bands seem to think that the people who follow them love their songs and are fans of their music. In some cases, this is true; however, most local groups just have followings, and very few bands have more than a handful of people who know and love their songs. Those fans are considered "true fans." Until your followers know your songs, can sing along to your songs, and love your songs, they're not really "true fans". They might be loyal followers, but how can they be true fans of your music if they are essentially unfamiliar with your songs?

Maybe these followers have heard your music, but again, if they can't sing or hum the chorus to any of your songs, then they are just a part of your following. This means that they are only coming to your shows to have fun. This isn't a bad thing. It doesn't mean that they don't like hearing your music. They may even love the way your music sounds. It just means that they are not coming to your shows for your songs. You must recognize that getting people to love your songs is critical to your group's long term success.

I know this can be confusing, especially for a band with a good following. Groups are obviously very familiar with their own songs and they usually love almost every single one of them. It's also human nature to see things from one's own perspective. The average band loves their own songs and they regularly see crowds of people that are enjoying their music, and so they assume that the crowd must like or love their songs or they wouldn't be there. What bands don't realize is that these people are not really familiar with any of their songs. Usually, these people have not been exposed to their songs sufficiently or in the right environment. A live setting is not the environment where people tend to fall in love with songs.

Local bands and national acts develop fan bases in different ways. The fans of a national act first hear a famous or soon-to-be-famous group's music on the radio or in some recorded fashion. Then, they come out to one of that group's shows, because they fell in love with a song they heard by that group.

Local groups don't usually have the luxury of airplay or anything even close to it. Local groups must first get people out to their shows, and then try to get those people to fall in love with their music and their songs. As you can see, these paths may seem very similar, but they are, in fact, completely different. The challenge with the local group's path is that it is a hundred times more difficult to get a bunch of people to fall in love with songs that they have only heard once or a few times in a live setting.

If someone is on the fence, but not ready to buy your music, then sweeten the deal. Offer to buy them a drink from the bar or to throw in a pair of tickets to your next show.

Converting Your Following into True Fans

The fastest way to grow in your market is to convert your loyal followers into fans of your songs. Frankly, the only way to convert a follower is first by getting them to *listen* to your songs. This is a challenge, even if you have recorded music, and it's almost impossible if you don't. Then, you must get them to like or hopefully love those songs. This will only work if you write songs that your followers enjoy. To get them to pay attention to your songs, you will most likely have to get them to buy your music. Obviously, for followers to buy your songs, you need to have your songs available for sale.

I have seen lots of bands give away their music in an effort to find new fans, and I do think there is value in this technique. However, in my experience, most people that are given free music throw it away or disregard it. How many times have you been given a free CD sampler and threw it away before you ever listened to a single track? Asking for money for your music is a critical component in getting someone to associate value with your music, which will increase the chances that they will listen to it. When you give something away, people generally assume it's because no one wants to buy it. If no one wants to buy it, why should they waste their time listening to it?

You need to receive money for your music while you're building a fan base for other psychological reasons. Once a person buys someone's music, they say certain things to themselves like, "Hey, I bought this CD, so I have to listen to it, I don't want to waste ten dollars." Or, "Hey, I must really like this group. I don't usually buy a local group's CDs." If a person sends the right message to their subconscious mind about your group, they become much more likely to listen to your music and to come to your next show.

Selling your music at your shows is probably more important than your actual performance, yet most groups passively sell their music at their shows. Usually at the last minute, they get a friend or a girlfriend to sell their CDs or T-shirts. Some even sell a few CDs themselves between playing their set and getting drunk (which usually leads to apathy and giving up on record sales). The fact is, the more music you can sell, the faster your fan base will grow and the more people you will convert from followers to true fans.

Your New Sales Team

The more music you sell, the more often the people buying your stuff will come out to see your group. As you convert followers into true fans, your sales team will grow. That's right: true fans become a sales force for your group as they wear your T-shirts around town. As they play your music in their cars and at parties for other potential true fans, your fan base grows further. We all love to be that guy or girl who knows about some great new band, and we love to tell everyone how we discovered them first. Convert your followers into true fans, and I promise they will tell everyone they know how great your bands is and how they found you first.

Now I say "true fans" instead of followers because these new fans will be coming from a different path than their predecessors. They will be coming not because you or someone you know asked them to come, but because they heard your music and they like or love it. In effect, you will be developing fans just like national acts do…with your recorded music first, instead of through a live performance. For the first time, you will start getting people at your shows that are fans of your music before they've ever seen you live.

It's Not Time to Record Your Masterpiece

At the local level, recording should not just be about putting out a record. It should be looked at as an opportunity to learn more about your craft. Whether you want to be a rock star or just make enough money so you can continue playing and creating music, you will need to become an expert in the process of recording. Writing and recording are the most important aspects of your musical career or future career.

Live music is great, but unless you're performing live at the super bowl half time show, it's very difficult to reach a lot of people at one time. When your music is recorded, it can be played on hundreds or thousands of radio stations around the world, on TV shows, or in movies. People can listen to your music while they sleep, or even while they're in the shower. Your recorded music is an important vehicle for your band—a vehicle that never rests.

Since recording is such a huge part of your career, you need to learn everything you can in order for you to master it. One of the best ways to learn anything is to get in there and just do it. I recommend that you get into a studio as fast as you can and start to put out small records. Put out small records, so you can easily recoup the expense of recording and then start working on your next release. This process will help you gain life experience while you turn your following into true fans by selling them your music.

Most groups go into the studio on their first attempt with the intention of recording their masterpiece. In reality, you're not likely to record your masterpiece on your first try in the studio. The problem with this intention is that most groups spend so much time and effort working to make that masterpiece that they never really get into the studio to record it. Have you found yourself in this situation? Don't procrastinate. Get into the studio, so you can start putting your music out there. The songs don't feel ready, or you don't feel ready? You don't have to be 100% ready, as long as you have prepared to the best of your ability for that moment in time. Get in there, and start recording. Once you're done, try to get back in the studio as often as possible. I call this The Write, Record, Release Method, and I discuss this important method in detail in the next Chapter.

Stop thinking in terms of perfection and start thinking in terms of progress and life experience. Perfection and talent come with experience and time. If you're so caught up in making things perfect that you never get into the studio, then you will prevent yourself from reaching the next level in your recording career. This will hinder your chances of ever making that masterpiece you so desire.

Establishing Credibility

Recording and putting out records is incredibly important. It gives you the kind of life experience you will need, something to sell, and a way for you to convert your following into true fans. It also gives your group credibility. With each release, your group will grow in size, as will your group's credibility. Now, when you or your manager get on the phone, he or she can talk about all of your records and how you've sold 2,000 units or more, and how you have a huge fan base in the area. Credibility goes a long way in this business. Make sure you get as much press as you can, sell as many records as possible, and draw as many people as you can to all of your shows. Do all of this, and you'll be on your way to becoming the biggest band in town, which is the best way to make it in the music business.

TIP: Constantly update your bio. Regularly add recent accomplishments and press clippings.

RECAP

- The more music you can sell, the faster your fan base will grow and the more people you will convert from followers to true fans.

- True fans become a sales force for your group, wearing your T-shirts and playing your music around tons of other people.

- Learn as much as you can about the recording process, because it's an integral component of your music career.

- Recording and releasing music will help you establish credibility in your market and in the industry.

CHAPTER 14

Releasing Albums

"I needed an opportunity to get back in the studio
and get my recording chops back together."

-Pat Travers

Albums are Tangible

In the beginning, people go to local shows just to have fun.
Then, after they buy a band's record (and if they like a song or two),
they'll start coming to shows to have fun *and* to hear the songs they
like. Yes, you can create a music scene around your band without ever
releasing a record, but it becomes so much easier after you have an
album available for sale. Once people can hear your music whenever
they want, and they can play it for other people, your group will have
reached a new level in your musical career. At this point, you will have
something to promote!

Remember that your band and your music are intangible and
hard to describe, making them hard to promote. But a CD is a tangible
product and much easier to promote. People can hold a CD in their

hands. If they put it in their CD player, they can listen to it. You must sell as many records as you can, and you need to try to get college or commercial airplay. You should send out promo units to the press and anyone else who you can help your career. Get every person you can to buy and to listen to your music.

Even digital copies of your album are tangible in the digital world. Your music is an attachment, or a link, or a stream. It's an online or mobile experience that could not be shared without a professional recording.

Normally, people go to see bands only after they fall in love with their music. In order to be truly successful in this business, you have to write great songs, and you have to get people to buy those songs. Until those songs become tangible (on an album), it is very difficult to sell your music at the local level. The cold reality is that people are not going to go onto the Internet and purchase your groups music—at least not in the beginning. You're going to need to use a lot of high-pressure salesmanship conducted by the best salesman you can find, or by the band itself. Having a tangible product that you can sell at your shows is the only practical way to sell your music.

 Record more songs than you plan to use on your record so you can put out the best album possible.

The Write, Record, and Release Method

The Write, Record, Release, Method means exactly that: you write about half a dozen songs, then you record them, and finally you release them in some sellable format. Then, you repeat the process. I recommend that you write somewhere between seven to ten songs, and then pick the best five or six songs to record. By recording a smaller number of songs, you can release smaller albums, which are called EPs. By releasing a smaller record, you can sell the record for less without devaluing your songs or your music. Since most of your followers are not yet fans of your songs, it's important to be able to sell them your records for less, without making people feel like your album is discounted out of some kind of flaw or lack of interest. Most people are a lot more comfortable spending $5-$7 for music that they are not familiar with, instead of spending $10-$15.

Because EPs require fewer songs, they allow you to spend less money in the studio, which makes the recording cost easier to raise and recoup. EPs are also easier to sell, because you can price them in that comfortable price range of $5-$7. Your music still retains its full value in the consumer's eyes, since you will be selling your EPs at full market value.

Now at this stage, you should have three goals:

1. To spend as little as possible recording and producing your record so you can quickly repeat the process. I recommend that you release an EP every six months.

2. To price the album so that you can sell as many CDs as possible. I recommend that you do everything you can to sell at least 300 units of your first record and a minimum of 500 units on your second release.

3. To gain experience, so your next recording session will produce better songs and a better sounding record. I recommend that you try to learn everything you can during the recording process.

You should release at least one record every year, but try to release one every six months. Imagine being in a band for two years and having four releases. People would certainly take you more seriously, and your life experience would help you to grow as a person and as a musician.

TIP: Create a plan that includes how your group will sell out your shows, and release at least two records per year.

Release Parties

Record release parties are not only one of the best ways to recoup all of the money you spent recording your record, but they're also a great way to expand your following and increase your number of true fans. Remember that a record release party can and should be used as a catapult event for your band. You should schedule and promote your record release party several months in advance. This is the most important thing you can do to guarantee a successful event, so give yourself a lot of time to promote it. And remember, when I say promote, I am really saying network. (Posting flyers on poles will not get it done.) Tell everyone you know and ask them to tell everyone they know to come to your party. The record release party is one of the *most* effective ways to grow your group, since most of your friends will come out to support you and attend your "party". It is at this point in which your group will start to build credibility in your hometown.

This is the kind of event that can change your band's image in the marketplace, and it happens to be one of the easiest ways for a band to make money, if properly planned. Try to work with a venue or promoter that will allow you to keep as much of the door money and presale tickets as possible. If you can make between $500 and $1,500 from the ticket sales, and then sell at least 100 CDs, you should be able to pay for most of your record, if not all of it. Your main goal should be to have an event that is so successful that you can recoup your entire investment.

I highly recommend that you sell advanced tickets to your record release party. You want to get everyone you know there, and the best way to ensure their attendance is by selling them a ticket. There are many ways to sell tickets, but as we have discussed, the best way is to get friends, family, and close fans involved.

First, get more tickets than you could ever sell. If you think the most you could sell is 100 tickets, then ask the promoter for 200. If you think you can sell 200 tickets, then ask for 300, and set your goal for 300 people. The higher your goal, the more interested others will be in coming to your show. Now here's your sales pitch:

"Hi, we're trying to get 300 hundred people to our record release party so we can sell it out. Will you help us with our dream?"

This does several things: first, it tells your potential customer that this is going to be a big, fun, crowded event—a party. Second, by coming, they're not only going to have a great time, but they're also helping you with your cause. Everyone loves causes.

If you're selling tickets before the CD cover and insert has been designed, you can tell people that if they buy a ticket, you will also thank them on the CD! This technique will help you sell not just one ticket to your show, but probably two or three tickets, as they will want to show their friends their name on your record. You also just guaranteed yourself another record sale. Take your 200-300 presale tickets and divide them amongst the members of your band. Then, each band member should divide them amongst their friends and family. Everyone should keep a list of who has what tickets. Most tickets are numbered, so this is easy to do.

> **People prefer to spend smaller amounts of money on unfamiliar music. Price your music accordingly.**

Next, create a huge industry guest list of over 500 people, as described in Chapter Six—the bigger the better! If you can come up with over 1,000 people, great! This list should consist of every music writer that works for every paper in town. Your list should include every person that works for the local music and arts paper; include the janitor, if you can get his or her name. Invite every DJ from every local radio station, commercial or college, as long as they play your style of music. Include every person from every recording studio in town, every promoter, club owner, and every person that works at every concert club in town. Go to every coffee shop, cool diner, music store and record store in your hometown and pass out invites and complementary tickets—one at a time.

Do as The AKT did: give every cool person that you meet who will not buy a ticket a free ticket—if they promise to use it. I usually make them think the guest list or the complimentary tickets are very limited or scarce, so the person receiving them feels special, and obligated to attend. All writers and DJs should also get an advanced copy of your music. You should ask all the DJs to play your record and ask all the writers to review it. For a complete list of people to invite, please review Chapter Six.

Make sure you do all of this at least 4-6 weeks before the night of your show. This time line is critical, as it will help you to create a buzz around your group and your show. Do it too late, and you will not be as effective in creating a buzz. From the day you booked your release party, start promoting it. Post the show on all of your networking sites, and get out there and tell everyone you know about the party. Have everyone in your band start making new friends daily and get people to commit to coming to your release party, ASAP. Make sure you're not playing anywhere else in town for at least six weeks before and after your release party, and do not promote anything else but this event!

After 70-100 tickets are sold, start telling people how many other people are coming. Tell them that you expect 300 just for your band plus another 300 from all the other bands. God helps those who hype themselves. Make fliers, and go out every night to network and tell people about your band. Go to every show where people who like your genre of music hang out. Show them your flyer and tell them about your group. Try to sell them a ticket! If they're not ready to buy, then get their ReverbNation information, their Facebook URL or email address, and develop the connection or relationship further. Keep talking to them about how many people you're expecting to come to your show. This is your record release party, so you need to do everything you can to pack the place. Keep in mind that the bigger the turn out for your release party, the better everyone will assume your record sounds. If you get a bad turn out, everyone there will assume the record is bad. If you sell out the venue, you will sell a lot more records for two reasons: first, you'll have more potential customers. Second, everyone's perception of your record will be a positive one, making the sale of your albums easier.

Selling Records

Use all of your efforts to sell as many records as you can at your release party and after your release party. Hire the best sales person you know— a few of them if you can—and get them to sell your EPs. Have them go around the room, make friends, sign fans up for your email list, and sell as many units of your music as possible. It is so important to sell records or some form of your music at every show and everywhere else. As you know, selling your music does several things for you.

Putting out an album and selling your music needs to be a focal point of your plan in reaching the next level. Anytime someone buys your music, it makes a deeper connection between your group and the fan that purchased it. The deeper the connection, the more likely they are to support your group by attending your shows more often. This is another reason you need to keep releasing music you can sell. Not only do you want to sell your music to as many people as possible, but you also want each fan to buy as much of your music as you can get them to buy. The more they buy, the deeper your connection with them will be.

 Recording an EP instead of a full album will allow you to spend less money in the studio, which makes the expense twice as simple to recoup.

When I was young, I had every Kiss record ever made, until they released the record "Unmasked." Up until that record, all I did was talk about Kiss all day long—my connection with their band was very strong. But after I stopped buying their records, I lost interest. You need to keep selling your music over and over to your current fans to keep them interested. When you see a local band that has huge local interest, and then they lose that interest, it is usually because they stopped selling their fans new music. Don't make the same mistake. Instead, keep writing, recording, and releasing new music.

RECAP

- Your band and music are intangible and therefore hard to promote; a CD is a tangible product and much easier to promote.

- Recording an EP instead of a full album will allow to you to spend less money in the studio

- You should release at least one record every year, but try to release one every six months.

- Schedule and promote your record release party months in advance.

STEP 5:
Create NAME RECOGNITION

CHAPTER 15

Airplay

"The radio makes hideous sounds. "

-Bob Dylan

Get on College Radio

College radio is a very approachable medium and it is easy to get your music played on college radio stations. Most college stations have a variety of musical formats that change by the day and by the hour. Every semester or at least once a year, they usually release a new program guide that will tell you who runs each program and what types of music each particular person plays during his or her radio show. Many groups even have friends that host their own radio shows on college radio. If don't have a friend at one of these college radio stations, have no fear… it's easy to make friends.

Get a program guide from each station within a 50-mile radius of your home base, and find out which stations and programs play your style of music. Then, call those stations during relevant shows to request songs and make friends with the people running them. College radio jocks are looking for an audience as badly as you are! Most times, they will play your songs in the hopes that you will continue to listen to their show. If possible, hand deliver, your music to each station so that everyone there that plays your style of music can have one. Then call weekly to request your music.

> **TIP:** Before you attempt to contact the stations in your area, make a list of every station you need to call. Then try to knock this out in one sitting. This way if you get rejected you can immediately get back on the horse.

You will be amazed at how easy this is for you to accomplish. After a few calls, you'll start hearing your songs on the radio without personally calling in to request them. When I was in the AKT, we were able to develop several friendships with different stations and even had one DJ interview us on the air. It was cool to listen back to the interview, as we had someone record it for us. Years later, that same DJ helped to run a local show on a commercial station in town and I was able to get him to play a few songs from another band that I was in at that time.

Try to make friends with all the college radio DJs and program directors at each station in town. See if you can get on the radio to give away tickets to all of your shows. Try to get at least one of the stations to sponsor your shows. They usually won't give you any money, but they can sometimes give you free announcements throughout the day. With their permission, you can use their call letters in all your advertisements. Then, you'll be able to tell everyone you know that a radio station is playing your songs. You'll be able to say that they like your music so much, they have agreed to sponsor your show. This will help make your events look bigger to your friends and fans, creating more interest for you and your band.

In return for their sponsorship, agree to give them 10-20 or more *pairs* of tickets to give away on air and let them have 10 or more pairs of tickets for their staff. Remember, it's all about getting people out to your shows. You want the coolest people that you can find there so they will attract other cool people as well. College DJs are usually considered cool: they get free tickets to concerts all the time and they are on the radio every week, or sometimes everyday. These are the kind of people you want at your shows, and you want as many of them as possible at every single show.

More College Radio

As you are making friends with people from the local college radio stations, pick their brains and ask them for help. They usually know which big concerts are coming to town, how certain trade magazines work, and other important people within the music community. For instance, they might be familiar with and have access to College Music Journal (CMJ). CMJ is a national publication that many people in the music industry read weekly.

CMJ is also one of the most important resources that you can use to grow your group. It lists all of the college radio stations around the country, and every week it shows how each artist is charting. Radio stations keep logs of every song they play; they take these logs and calculate which songs get the most plays. College Music Journal and other publications or agencies collect these logs and publish the results. Now, if you have gotten a hold of every jock at every college radio station that plays your kind of music in town and they are playing your songs, then your group is going to start charting in CMJ.

College radio program directors and commercial radio stations reference CMJ to see what's happening in the industry. It helps them determine which artists they should consider playing based on who else in the country is playing what music by whom. CMJ is an expensive subscription, but if you can make the right connections, then you might be able to get your hands on an older issue. People tend to look them over and then disregard them after the next issue arrives. The publication is now also available online, which means you might be able to peek at their charts online with the right help. With this source, you can find out who the program directors are all over the country for every station that charts in CMJ.

Once you have this information, you need to send every program director from every city that you would like to target your press kit and CD. I recommend that you target regions where you have toured or where you can easily tour in the future. You should contact regions or markets where you have some kind of connection. For example, if someone in your band used to live in a certain city, then I suggest you target that region. You can use the fact that someone from your band is originally from that area as a hook.

Your music needs to get other peoples attention, that's why *hooks* are so important. When your band needs to get other peoples attention use the same formula *hooks*—a reason why your group is special or a reason why they should play your music. The better the hook, the more likely someone will play one of your songs. Touring in a certain region regularly or in the future is one of those hooks. Hip-Hop artists are constantly working with other big artists, and this is another great hook. If your group recorded a few songs with a producer or in a studio in a particular city, you have a hook. You should come up with dozens of hooks to convince stations to play your music. The more hooks you have, the better your chances are of getting airplay.

Send your music and bio out to your targeted program directors. After they have had time to receive your package (digitally or physically), start calling them. Start your conversations by making friends with them. Make friends by using your hook or hooks—tell them how you are connected to their region, or their station. If your hook is that your bass player went to college in that city, then open with: "Hi Tom, I understand that you are the program director at WCSB. Our bass player, Eric, went to school there. He always talks about how he misses your station. I was wondering if you got the package I sent you with our music and bio? We would really love it if you would give it a listen and tell us which DJs might be interested in our music." Don't be afraid to ask for the names of the DJs that play your genre of music and when those programs air. Get their names, so you can send each one of them your music. Then after a week, call all of them, too.

Every week, try to get the old copies of CMJ and see where you are charting. Call the program directors again and tell them where you are charting around the country. As your record starts gaining momentum, continue to tell the program directors about your group and your success—the more you can tell them about yourself, the more likely they will be to play your music even more. You need to stay in touch so that your band is on their minds all of the time; if they forget about you, they will also forget about your record.

Ask other bands in town who they know at the local college radio stations. See if they will let you name drop, making your first contact even more comfortable.

Get on Commercial Radio

Once you are successful in the college market, and you chart on twenty or more stations nationally, then it's time to start calling your local commercial radio stations. Try to set up meetings with local program directors. Send them emails on how you are charting on over 20 college stations around the country. Ask them to sponsor your next show. Email them proof that you are charting. Keep in mind that the more stations you chart on in the college market, the more interested they will be in your band. Once you get their ear, ask them what it would take to get them to play one of your songs. Even if it's only on their weekly local show, it will really help your band.

If your group is charting on college radio and getting spins on commercial stations, your bio is going to look really solid. While you are improving your bio and making important friends, do everything you can to get your local commercial radio station's attention and respect. It's going to be an uphill battle that will rarely result in airplay, but do what you can to get on their radar.

Once you have their attention, they will start thinking of your band whenever opportunities come up for local support on radio-sponsored concerts. Your group needs to be at the top of everyone's list for favorite local group in your area. If a record company rep comes to town to meet with radio station personnel and asks, "Who's the best local band in town?" You want the answer to be you!

Regardless of whether or not you can get your music on the radio, start making friends and invite the whole station down to your shows. If they show up, treat them like royalty and make sure you impress the hell out of them with your performance. They might not be able to play your music on their station for business or financial reasons. However, these people work and talk with important people almost daily—these people have the power to change your life forever, make friends with them. Keep going, keep networking your way to the top.

If you're able to chart on twenty or more college radio stations, and you are able to get a few of your local commercial radio stations playing your songs, then you're definitely on the right path. Keep the buzz going with college radio by continuing to call them each week, and continue searching for other stations that will add your song to their playlists. Get new stations interested by telling them who else just started playing your hit song that week. You can also tell them how many stations are playing it, or that it charted #1 on a certain station or stations.

Once you reach this stage, you should start looking for someone to help you go after airplay immediately. Look into smaller labels that are getting their artists airplay or hire a company that specializes in helping bands get on commercial radio. Understand that this is difficult and that you're probably going to get rejected at every corner. Be strong, and keep in mind that what you're really trying to do at this point in your career is to build relationships and get noticed by people that can help you. It doesn't matter so much whether they play your song, just that they now know you, your band and music.

RECAP

- Try to make friends with all the college radio DJs and the program directors at each station you can.

- Stay in touch with radio personnel so that your band is on their minds all of the time. If they forget about you, they will also forget about your record.

- Do everything you can of to get your local commercial radio station's attention and respect.

CHAPTER 16

Get Press

"It's amazing that the amount of news that happens in the world every
day always just exactly fits the newspaper."

-Jerry Seinfeld

Most News Stories Are Placed News

Where does news come from? Well...most stories are placed
news, meaning someone told the paper about a story or sent a press
release to announce something to the press. If the editor finds the
press release interesting, then he or she will assign a writer to work on
the story. Newspapers and other media, get more press releases than
they could ever write stories about. If a press release contains so much
compelling, interesting information that the article almost writes itself,
then your chance of getting coverage goes up. You want your press
releases to be informative and as interesting as possible. Controversy,
scandal, and drama usually attract readers. Readers attract advertisers,
and advertisers pay the bills. Try to make your press releases as juicy as
possible, and fill them with lots of interesting information. It's like

writing hit songs or getting a program director's attention—you need a hook. Once you have their attention, you can tell them the rest of your story, and they will listen.

If a writer thinks there might be a big story, or the paper happens to be low on news that particular week, they might call you to get more information. Always be prepared to give them more information, and use this opportunity to build a relationship with that writer and his or her paper. It's so important to build relationships with everyone you can. Building relationships with the press should be at the top of your list.

A few years ago, a good friend of mine, Joe, and I were training for a triathlon called "Escape from Alcatraz." We trained for months. We even went swimming in Lake Erie in late October for training purposes. Now, if you're not from Ohio, you might not know how cold the lake is in October. It's really cold!—in the low 50's, at most. While this is not newsworthy on an average day, we happened to catch the media's attention on this day. We were on the beach getting ready to go into the lake, when a photographer approached us to ask what we were doing. He wanted to know why we were swimming in the lake at this time of year. He thought we were crazy or something. As it turned out, he worked for the newspaper. Since it was a slow news week, the paper sent him out looking for a story. When he saw us, he asked us a few questions and took a few pictures of us swimming. The next day we were in the paper.

In addition to having a newsworthy story, you sometimes need to have good timing as well. You might have a great story for the paper, but if it happens to be the same week that Michael Jackson died, then you're probably not going to make the paper. Stay at it and find every reasonable opportunity to get press as you can—I say reasonable because if you start sending press releases out every time you have to run to the bathroom, you're going to lose credibility with the paper and they're going to start ignoring you.

Record release parties are great opportunities to send out press releases. If your group is about to tour or record with someone famous, then you have a hook and should send out a press release. Remember to always follow up each press release with a phone call. See if they have room for your story or if they need any more information. Always try to build a relationship.

Press Releases

Getting press is a lot like getting airplay, except it's easier. Radio stations usually deal with a certain number of people. Newspapers are used to getting news from just about anyone. The best way to reach any newspaper is through press releases, which follow certain rules and are formal in nature. I recommend that you either research the proper way to format a press release or hire someone that knows how to write one. You can also find a lot of information on the internet on writing a proper press release. We have examples of press releases on our website at **www.gorillamusic.com**. Please feel free to use the same format that we have provided. You will just need to add your own content.

As I stated, the more interesting and appealing you make your press release, the more likely the press will use it and write something about your group. The title should grab the reader's attention, much like a newspaper headline. Make sure the first 8-10 words of the release are effective in conveying your message. Try to deal with facts instead of fancy words or language. It is also important to include as much contact info as possible. Make sure the press release is well written and grammatically correct. It needs to look as professional as possible in order for them to take you seriously. If you cannot afford to pay someone to help you write and edit a press release, then have a well-educated friend or family member help you with it. I cannot understate the importance of professionalism and proper formatting or your press releases.

Write more than one press release at a time. Come up with at least 10 topics for your releases. Pick the best one and send it out to at least 10 nearby papers

Send It Everywhere

Once you have written your press release, I recommend that you send it out to every paper within a 50-mile radius of your home base and/or wherever the story is relevant. Send it to weekly papers and daily papers; send it to music, entertainment, and internet publications. You should send it everywhere. The more people that you can get to write about you, the better. Again, after you send out your press release, make follow up calls to each paper. Ask if they have received it, and ask them to write something about your band. Offer to talk directly to the writer in charge of writing your article, or to send him or her more information.

Once they write something, create your next exciting story and send out another press release to everyone. Every time you send a press release out, make follow up calls and try to develop friendships with editors, writers, and anyone else that works for the paper. Build a media list. Remember to keep networking your way to the top. Getting to know writers and editors is an important part of that process. It's important that you continue to increase the number of people and magazines or newspapers that you're sending press releases out to each month. Your goal should be to send out at least one press release to all of your contacts every 6-8 weeks.

Another good topic to use for a press release is to announce your next record release. Discuss how you're having a record release party at such and such club next month, and why it's going to be so exciting. Include info like how your last show sold out, or how every local VIP in town attended it. Name names and take pictures. A picture is worth a thousand words, especially if you want someone to print your article. If someone famous attends your show, make sure you take a picture with that person. If you do, you're going to have a huge hook for the press. Everyone who reads the article or sees the photo will forever associate your group with that celebrity.

 Get the paper's attention by sending them something unusual. When our group sent out our first press release with a song called "Broken Glass," we sent pieces of glass along with our music.

After you schedule your next show, and you start working on getting people there, invite everyone that works at every paper in town. Always try to network and to make influential friends everywhere you go and every time you're promoting your group and your group's shows.

I touched on this in Chapter Two: the over-kill method. In my days with The AKT, we sent a few of our best songs out to every writer from every paper in town. For the bigger papers in town, we also sent invites to every single person that worked there. We sent invites to the writers, the editor, everyone in the advertising department, all of the graphic designers, and even the receptionist. If someone's name was listed as an employee of that paper, then we invited them, regardless of their position.

When you invite everyone from the paper, the people that never get invited anywhere start asking questions. They are usually flattered or confused—both are good for your group. As they go around the office asking everyone about you, it creates a buzz amongst the employees about your group. How often do you think the people at your local newspaper go around talking about local bands all day? Yeah, NEVER! Use this technique, and they'll be talking about *you*. They might joke around the office about how you sent the 57 year old guy in accounting that hates music an invite to a rock concert, but what they say doesn't matter. What matters is that they're talking about you, and your chances of getting them to write about you just skyrocketed.

Every single time that I have used this technique, I have gotten an article written about my band or the band I was working with at that time. In one case, we were made fun of in the paper for sending some old guy an invite to a show that he had no interest in attending. I just smiled as I thought to myself, "It worked." "We just got a full page article with our band's photo in the most important paper in town."

Like I stated in Chapter Six, "Sell Out Your Shows," sell tickets to anyone who will buy a ticket from you and give tickets to every person who won't buy a ticket in the hopes that they might come after all.

People who work for newspapers and magazine usually get into concerts for free, so they might be insulted if you ask them to buy a ticket. This is especially true, if you're hoping for a review. You want and need them there, so put them on the guest list or give them free tickets. Do whatever you have to do to get them there.

Send Your Music, Too

Don't just send a press release. You also need to send them your music. These days, it's easy to send a press release and an electronic sample of your music. Send a press release with at least one of your songs and try to tie that press release to that song, so that they are more likely to listen to it. Make it your goal to get them to listen to your music and to comment in their article on your music. It's difficult to describe the way a group's music sounds in print. Having a written testimonial can help you impress your current following, local venues, other bands, and important VIPs in the music business. It also provides you great material for your bio and press kit. In addition, if someone is looking for something different to do that weekend and they respect a certain writer's opinion, maybe you'll get lucky and you'll pick up a new fan—not because your name was in the paper or because you sound like you might be a cool band, but because of the reader's respect for that writer's opinions. It's just like when one of your fans brings a friend along to see your group.

Advertise

Advertising is a tricky subject since, for the most part, a print ad cannot directly help an unknown artist gain fans or get new people to their shows. Frankly, neither will an article in the newspaper. So, you're probably wondering why I just spend most of this chapter explaining how to get press for your group.

There are ways to use advertising and press to help build your events, and your band. Yes, no one outside of your social circle knows who you are, so traditional marketing is mostly ineffective. A print ad will fail miserably in any attempt to attract new fans on its own, but it can dramatically improve your chances of getting your current fans out to one of your events.

Placing an ad in your local paper or alternative weekly, and making sure that your entire fan base knows about the ad, can really create a strong buzz within your social circle. This buzz creates a ripple effect, as your social circle has even more reason to reach out to the people in their social circles to talk about your band and your upcoming event. Remember, people want to go to local shows to have fun. If your group is already drawing a healthy crowd and your fans see that you're heavily advertising one of your shows, their natural reaction will be to think, "Wow, this is going to be big! I can't miss this event!" It's crucial to make the event as big as possible and to let everyone know how big your event is going to be in terms of attendance and importance. When they see your ad, they will know that you're a serious group. Then the buzz begins. You want that buzz to be as big as possible, so do everything you can to fan the flames of that buzz.

In addition to creating a buzz within your social circle, a print ad will also help you to get the newspaper's attention and to get them to take your group more seriously. Most newspapers will tell you that their advertising department and their editorial department are two completely separate divisions, and one doesn't affect the other. That might be true in most cases, but when a local band starts advertising in their paper, it will draw attention to that group. It's not intentional on the part of the paper, but they can't help but notice, because it's unusual, which is good for you. Frankly, the fact that your group is advertising in the paper is newsworthy in itself, which is one of the reasons they'll notice you. This attention is going to get you more press, and more press is good for your press kit and bio. Plus, it will continue to impress your local following.

If your following sees an article on your band and an impressive print ad in the paper, then their perception of your band will inflate. Since it's almost unheard of for local groups to run print ads, your followers will assume that your group is now reaching the next level.

Once they make this assumption, they are going to want to be a part of that success by attending more of your shows, buying more of your music, and hoping that they get to know you better or talk to you at one of your shows. Your followers will tell people that "their" band is in the paper. Can you see how this starts to create a buzz?

The ad on its own doesn't help get anyone new to come out to see you. However, it can get your fans more excited to tell everyone about your band, which will help bring new people to your show. Print ads and stories help your group to build name recognition in the market, which is an important step in your growth as a local band. But make sure you understand how this advertising campaign works. If you run an ad in the local paper and you don't tell anyone about the ad, it will not help your shows or your band. For this technique to work, you must run an impressive, professional-looking ad, and you must tell everyone you know about the ad in the paper Take a photo of your ad and share it online. If your fans don't see the ad (or aren't aware of the ad), it will not energize them. If they're not excited about the ad, it will not be effective in getting them to your show or getting them to bring people to your show.

The number of followers you have will play a big role in how much a print ad will help your shows. I do not recommend buying a print ad if you have a small fan base and very few friends. Running a print ad or getting an article in the paper is only going to engage your current fans, not create new ones—at least not without the help of your current fans. Therefore, if you don't have any fans, do not run a print ad. It will not work for your band. However, if you have a big fan base, then you should start to consider the use of print ads for your next event. The bigger your current fan base, the better the results will be from this sort of advertising tactic.

Growing a local band is about great songs, having outstanding live shows, increasing your group's social circle through networking, growing a strong base of genuine fans, and creating name recognition in the market so you can continue to grow. As your group's name builds in the market place, it becomes easier for your fans to convince others to come out and see your band. That's what you need: an army of true fans singing your praises to the rest of the world.

RECAP

- Record release parties are great opportunities to send out press releases.

- Every time you send a press release, make follow up calls and try to develop friendships with editors, writers, and anyone else that works for the paper.

- Send a press release with at least one of your songs and try to tie that press release to that song, so they are more likely to listen to it.

- If you run an ad in the newspaper and you don't tell anyone about the ad, it will not help your shows or your group.

CHAPTER 17

Opening for National Acts

"God helps those who help themselves."

-Benjamin Franklin

Who is in Charge?

Getting a chance to open for a famous touring act is an important opportunity. Unfortunately, these kinds of gigs are hard to find and almost impossible to obtain beyond the club circuit. Bands that are considered for these opportunities usually know someone in charge. Even if they know someone, there still has to be room on the show and it has to make economic sense before someone will consider adding them as local support. All the parties also need to agree (or at least not care much) about the presence of local talent. Getting this done can be a challenge since the various parties involved with most concerts frequently have different interests.

The first party is the band that's touring. They generally want to sell-out their concerts in order to make more money and to move up the ladder. They also want to keep their integrity intact and put on the best show possible for their fans. They will sometimes request that a certain band opens for them, and they typically have first say on who does. Some touring acts put a great deal of thought into the line-ups for their shows, and some groups don't care who opens up for them, as long as the act doesn't hurt or interfere with the production. If you're fortunate enough to have a relationship with a headlining band that makes every decision regarding their shows, and they want you on their show, then you're as good as in. However, if you're not friends with a band that is fussy about openers, then it's going to be an uphill battle.

Groups that have no interest in their openers will often leave that decision up to their booking agent or their management. These bands still have control of their shows, if they want it. Making friends with them can also get you the spot—assuming that the band wants to help you out. Therefore, the best situation you can have regarding these premium opportunities is to be friends with, or have some kind of relationship with the headlining band.

Management is usually next in line in the decision-making process regarding opening acts. The band's manager basically has the same opinion on the subject as the band. Unless they have another group that they manage, or they owe someone a favor, they don't usually care who opens as long as their artist is happy. If you know someone who manages the band that you want to open for, you may have a good chance at getting on that show. Most managers and groups have strong relationships, and groups will consider the manager's opinion. Therefore, the manager can make a good case for your band, and hopefully get you on the bill.

Third in line is the talent agent, who is the person or the company that books a group's dates and tours. Most talent agents care about two things—their artist's best interests and making money. Everyone has to prosper in the short and long term, so the agents can keep their jobs. Talent agents frequently owe more favors to people and have more artists under contract than managers. This causes them to want to put their own clients on important shows and tours. If you're not from

L.A. or N.Y.C., then you're probably not going to know any talent agents personally. If you do, or if you can build a strong bond with an important agent who wants to open some doors for you, then you can get your band on a ton of great shows. Agents, although third in line, end up putting together and controlling a good number of the line ups for most tours. Most bands really don't put a lot of thought into anything outside of their own performance while touring. They end up leaving those details to their agent, who is expected to use those slots to enhance the sell-ability of the tour and drive ticket sales. Bigger attendances mean more money next time out, and that's critical for any band wanting to grow. If they can accomplish these goals with one of the other bands on their roster or with someone to whom they owe a favor, they will.

In most cases, the promoter or venue owner is last in line when it comes to selecting opening acts. This is unfortunate for local groups, because venue owners and promoters are the parties that are most interested in having local support on their events. Their interests are to make the agents they buy shows from happy, to make their ticket buying customers happy, to make the bands they book happy, and to make money and stay in business. The order of these interests differs depending on how well a show is selling. If a show is selling well, then making the agent and the headlining band happy is priority number one. If the show is doing poorly and the band is receiving a big guarantee, then money becomes the biggest concern. When this happens and a club owner or promoter is on the line for big bucks, promoters will scramble to find any way to fix the show. If your band can *be* that fix by selling loads of tickets for them, then you're going to have a better chance of getting on that show. The promoter will need to convince the other parties—or at least the headliner's agent—that the addition of your group to the bill will benefit everyone.

The best way to get shows opening for national acts is by befriending the venues in town.

Who Has The Power?

Even though bands usually have the first say as to whom the openers are on their shows, the venue/promoter ultimately has all the power. Since they're the ones paying for and hosting the show, they can often put pressure on the headliner to allow local openers on the show, especially if the show is bombing. However, the promoter has to be willing to flex their muscles in order to have that power. Generally, they won't push for it, because competition is high for the best shows. The top talent agencies pull all the strings in the concert industry. Most clubs are afraid to burn any bridges for fear that they will lose future opportunities.

Some of the stronger and smarter promoters have realized that they have the power, and so they will use every technique they can to get local support on their national shows. They know that a few good-drawing local groups can reduce their risk and make a better event for everyone. This can only happen though, if it makes economic sense. To be considered as one of top local groups, you will need to make an impact on ticket sales to have any chance at playing on one of these shows. Bringing 50-100 people to a show at a venue that holds 15,000 people makes no sense at all. In fact, the cost of having you on a show like that would be thousands of dollars. Selling 50-100 tickets would hardly be enough to offset the staging costs. However, bringing 50-100 people to a 500-capacity concert club is a completely different story, and it makes perfect sense. It's good for everyone involved, as long as the opening group is in the same genre, decent sounding, and will help sell-out the show (or at least positively impact the attendance of the show).

We already know that the better attended the show, the more fun the headliner's fans will have there. Adding another band also adds to the length of the show, which brings more value to the venue (bar sales) and hopefully to the ticket-buying fans. If the venue does well, they can offer the headliner more money on their next trip through town, which helps everyone associated with that artist.

Where and How to Align Yourself

Aligning yourself with an influential talent agent can bring you the most value, but they're pretty far up the food chain and hard to reach. Getting in good with a touring act or a well-connected band manager that's already having some success would also be of great value, but until you get to play with them or in front of them, it's hard to make that connection. The venue or local promoter is the easiest person with whom you can align your group. In fact, making this connection is pretty easy, especially if your band has been selling out shows with that promoter for a while. If you have been working with the promoter and doing a great job bringing people to your shows, then he already knows that you can help ticket sales.

If your group can bring a few hundred people out to your shows, you will generate a lot of pull within your market, which will give you the advantage to negotiate these opening slots. If the venue you work with most doesn't help you to get on good shows, then you might want to consider taking your sold-out shows elsewhere. Frankly, if your group is drawing big crowds, and the venue or promoter isn't nurturing your career in some way, you should consider going elsewhere. They can help your group by making sure that your shows are better, exposing you to the media, introducing you to industry contacts, giving you good dates, or by paying you favorably. Helping you to open for national acts is one of those things a good venue can offer you, but only if your band has worked hard and is drawing a few hundred people.

Some promoters are going to have a harder time convincing talent agents to let local support on their shows, while other promoters may have more power and can get what they want from the agents. Try to align yourself with a powerful promoter, or at least a crafty one, who can sneak a few bands on their shows without much trouble.

When my co-author Dan owned Peabody's, he was a genius at getting local support on national shows. He would put bands on these shows with a certain understanding. If the headliner showed up and got upset about the extra acts, he would have to take them off of the show. The club would have the local openers sell as many tickets as possible for that show. On the day of the show, as soon as the headliner pulled up to the club, Dan would stop everything he was doing to meet all the people on the crew and all the band members. He would make friends with everyone, offering them some drinks and pizza or something like that. He would make sure that they got everything on their rider, even if he went over budget, which always happened.

By the time the headliner found out that there were other bands on the bill, they were already enamored with Dan. He had already done more for their group than any other club on the entire tour. Most of them would ignore the fact that Dan had a few extra bands on the show. Anyone that did get upset would change their tune when they found out that the openers sold a ton of tickets. Often times, the opening acts were the reason that the show sold out or reached back-end points. This means that the headliner would be getting more money than what they were guaranteed, all thanks to the opening acts.

TIP: Use your ReverbNation account to make friends with bands that are touring. This is especially important if you're going to be opening for them in your town.

Most promoters will try to cut the overhead of the show by cutting the band's budget for food and by padding their expenses so they can make as much off the door as possible, leaving nothing for the band except their guarantee. Dan did the opposite: he gave all the bands everything on their rider and more, and then did everything he could to make sure that when the band left, they made more money on their show with him than anywhere else on the tour. The agents and the bands loved him for this and would tell him all the time that they couldn't believe how much more money he paid them than anyone else, even if he had to eat a few extra expenses to make it happen. This was important, since most groups need every penny they can get to keep their costs down and get to the next town. Many touring acts at the club level barely break even and need their record label's financial support in order to tour; this is called tour support. It's important to know that any support from a label needs to be paid back before a group can make a profit.

Dan knew which headliners would allow him to get away with squeezing in local acts, and he also knew which headliners to not try this on. He also made sure that the additional local acts would not affect the headliner's performance time or sound check. Most headliners could hardly tell there were any other bands on the show until they hit the stage. By then, the room was so full that it turned out to be the best show on their whole tour. Headliners always left the venue with smiles on their faces and a whole lot more money than they expected. They loved playing a great show with a promoter who treated them like kings all day long. It's no wonder that all those bands and talent agents enjoyed working with Dan, and still do today.

To my knowledge, Dan has only miscalculated one time. He once booked a headliner that refused to allow the additional openers. To solve this, he separated the shows and moved all of the local bands playing on that same night to a different venue. He then reduced the price of any tickets sold to people who didn't want see the national band—the people that only bought tickets to support their friend's band. At first, the local openers were terribly disappointed, but this attitude changed when they discovered that their show still kicked ass. The local bands ended up selling out the other venue and having the time of their lives. The local show was bigger than the national act's show, which was quite embarrassing for that national act.

Impressing the Wrong People

Once a local band lands an opening slot on a big national act concert, they start to prepare. They often go around and tell everyone they know about the show, which is very beneficial, but they usually misunderstand the opportunity. I can't tell you how many bands seem to think that all the fans of the headliner are somehow going to instantly love their group too. Some are crazy enough to think that their group is somehow going to get a better response form the crowd than the headliner on the night of the show. I've heard groups say things like, "We're going to blow them away," in reference to the nationally touring act. First of all, that's not realistic. People rarely if ever fall in love with a group after seeing one live performance, especially if they've never heard that group's music before. Secondly, it's not their fans you want to impress. Yes, you should try your best to impress everyone, including the headliner's fans. After your performance, you should try to network with everyone at that show by selling your group's merchandise and signing everyone up on your email list. However, there are bigger fish to fry with these precious opportunities.

At the local level, growing in the music business is not really about promoting, but instead, networking. The most important reason you want to be on these shows is to become friends with the national acts that you're opening for that night. You don't want to blow them away—you want to impress them, to make them fall in love with your group. You want them to start talking about you, to take you on the road under their wing, and to introduce you to their management team and label. You want to learn from them and develop a *life-long* friendship with them and everyone around them.

This is the actual value in these types of show opportunities—not in trying to impress a few hundred people who have no clue who you are. Most of the headliner's fans have little interest in finding out anything more about your band. They simply want your set to end, so they can see the headliner they paid to see. Now don't get me wrong, you want to impress as many people as you can with your performance, as that will make a positive impression on the headliner. If you sell enough tickets that the place goes crazy when you hit the stage, the headliner's fans will suddenly become very interested in what's going on. You might also sell a bunch of shirts and CDs, and win over a few followers that eventually become true fans. Of course, you should work the crowd once your performance is over and try to sell as much merchandise as you can. Hit every one of them up with your T-shirts, your music, and your mailing list, and do not take no for an answer. Sell, Sell, Sell!

TIP: To get labels interested in your band, sell lots of records at the local and regional level.

Opening for national acts can be one of the fastest ways you grow your group. It's a giant step toward getting out of your hometown and getting your group noticed. To maximize this opportunity, you need to help the national act sell out their show, stay out of their way regarding set times and sound check, and then—most importantly—make friends with them. The best way to do that is to just be yourself and act in a friendly, professional manner, while bringing value to them on the day of the show.

RECAP

- The best way to open for a national act is to be friends with or have some kind of relationship with the headliner.

- Even though the bands usually have the first say as to whom the openers are on their shows, the club ultimately has all the power.

- If your group is drawing big crowds, venue or promoter should be helping you to further your career.

- Opening for national acts can be one of the fastest ways you grow your group.

CHAPTER 18

Record Labels

"I signed with an independent label, Continuum. After that, I put out a totally independent record, sold fourteen thousand of them from my basement, bought a house, started raising my kid, and made a decent living."

-Kid Rock

What Do Labels Want?

A record company is a business; just like any other business, one of their main objectives is to make money. Without this objective, their chances of survival are low, since running a business takes money. Every legitimate business has overhead, rent, staffing, office expense, utilities and taxes; lacking financial success makes it impossible to pay these expenses.

In the recent past, record companies made much more money than they do today. Illegal pirating has been the cause of most record label's financial problems, and with these struggles, the landscape of the music business has changed. If you're looking for a record deal now, then you need to understand how these changes affect you and your plans. Until a few years ago, labels were signing artists based mostly on their ability to write great songs. If they thought that your group had great songs that were capable of getting the world's attention, then they were interested in your band. Having great songs was the number one criteria for a band to get a record deal. But now that's changed.

Labels used to burn through money like crazy signing loads of potential groups, hoping to get at least one star out of each bunch they signed. I once heard that record companies only needed 1 of 26 groups to pop in order for them to make a profit. If they were able to find that one star, then it would pay for all of the other groups that had failed. That sounds like a very bad business model to me. So even if the industry finds a way to stop the things that are damaging their business and their companies, I would not expect them to return to that formula.

Labels cannot afford to take the same kinds of risks they took in the past. The potential upside is not what it was in the 80s, 90s, and early 2000s. Back then, there were artists selling millions of records at the drop of a hat; Michael Jackson's "Thriller" has sold over 65 million records. Today, the biggest selling artist of the year sells maybe three or four million records. In both the years 2002 and 2010, Eminem was the biggest selling artist of the year. In 2010, he sold 3.4 million records— half as many as he did in 2002, when he sold 7.6 million. When labels lost their huge upside, they were forced to cut costs and reduce their risk. Now they want groups that have proven that they can sell music.

How to Get a Record Deal

Record companies are looking for groups that are already succeeding—that are already selling records on their own. They don't want to take chances; they want artists with proven track records. They want artists that can limit their risk, but also have huge potential. If your group is an experimental sounding band with little to no fan base, your chances of getting a deal are going to be much slimmer than a group that's already touring efficiently and effectively, has a strong fan base, and has already started selling records on their own.

TIP: If you're serious about a career in the music business, then put your heart and soul into your music and your shows.

What if you were in their shoes? Let's say you sold everything you owned and started your own label. Would you rather work with some group that doesn't have any experience, doesn't seem to have any fans in their hometown, and hasn't sold any of their own music? Or on the other hand, would you rather work with a group that is already up and running, has a huge local fan base, great songs, and a great live show, and has sold a bunch of records on their own?

The best way to get a record deal is to follow these 5 Steps:

1. Write Great Songs	**S**	Songs
2. Create outstanding live shows	**O**	Outstanding Shows
3. Create name recognition in the market	**N**	Name Recognition
4. Make genuine connections with fans	**G**	Genuine Fns
5. Turn your social circle into a huge fan base	**S**	Social Circle

Start by turning your social circle into a massive fan base. As your fan base grows, all the right people will hear about your group. As a former club owner, I regularly saw this happen right before my eyes. Groups that have 100-person fan bases get the attention of every club in town; bands that have a 200-person draw or more start to get interest from venues in neighboring cities. Once a group grows to have a 500-person fan base in their hometown and can draw a few hundred people in a few other markets, then the important folks in L.A. and N.Y.C. start to grow interested. So grow locally, then regionally, playing sold out shows and selling records along the way. If your group has 300-500 people coming out to all of your shows in a 5-10 market region somewhere in the US, and you have sold five to ten thousand records on your own, then every label around will be interested in your group. Once everyone is interested, you're going to be able to negotiate the best deal possible for your group.

Where to Start?

Start in one market—your home market—and grow fan by fan until your shows are packed. Use all your efforts to get as many people as you can to every one of your shows. Do this by networking habitually, dragging people to your shows, and booking your shows properly. While you're networking, start writing songs that have the ability to get the world's attention and find ways to connect with your fans on a personal or genuine level. Get your name out there by generating press for your band, by getting college airplay, and by meeting as many important industry people as you can meet. And last but not least, make sure you have outstanding live shows that Rock Your City.

RECAP

- Record companies are looking for groups that are already selling records on their own.

- Grow locally, then regionally, playing sold out shows and selling records along the way.

- Remember: **S.O.N.G.S.**

John and Dan would like to thank:

The Stankewicz Family	Kelly Statham	Ray Hunter
Cindy Carlsen	John Jones	Tim Caskey
Michael Carlozzi	Richard Patrick	Frank Vale
Dave Salay	Stacy Painter	Richard Piece
Sime Gelo	Jeremy Burkhamme	Chris Demkow
Jim Stafford	Geo Jones	Michelle Belleau
Brandon Lazano	Josh Kabat	Kirk Sommer
David Chidekel	Jeff Blue	Lou Plaia
Josh Lefkovitz	Rob Dippold	Jamie Adler
Jay-Z	Dave Kirby	Andrew Goodfriend
John Finburg	Richard Kabat	Chris Zitterbart
Packy Malley	Sir Richard Branson	Ron Opaleski
Kevin Lyman	Eric Fermin	Craig Mogil
Charles Attal	Dominic Pandiscia	Alan Becker
Ron Spaulding	Seymour Stein	Shep Goodman
Jeff Peters	Monte Conner	Nick Ferrara
Dave Rath	Jacob Fain	Mike Faley
Jen Graham	Anthony Brummel	John Weakland
Ian Cripps	Maria Gonzalez	Thomas Dreux
Rika O'Connor Gargano	Paul Gargano	Evan Peters
Ian Friedman	Ash Avildsen	Danny Vega
Kevin Zinger	Britton Kimler	Chuck Bernal
Mike Monterulo		

Andrew Ellis	Matt Galle	Ginny Song
Craig Newman	Ken Fermaglich	Dave Kaplan
Steve Kaul	Seth Rappaport	David Galea
Andrew Buck	Tom Windish	Robby Fraser
Armond Sadlier	Mark Whitford	Michael Yerke
Ron Petterson	Jason Miller	Dave Thomas
Stephen Rehage	Paul Ash	Doug Simmons
Bo Matthews	John Benson	Anastasia Pantsios
Mike Shea	Bill Peters	Roger Ganley
Jim Wadsworth	Tyler Lombardo	Troy Nethken
Mark O'Shea	Trent Weller	Brandon Zano
Ben Schigel	Mike Brown	Marty Geramita
Derek Hess	Columbus Woodruff	Pants Sechrist
Lisa Vinciquerra	Latif Hughes	Sasha Kulic
Daniel Thiel	Lee Frankel	Nick Storch
Miles Copeland	Steve-O	Jenny McPhee
Cara Lewis	Travis O'Guin	Hank LoConti
Scott Fraiser	Anthony Nicolaidis	Michael Belkin
Kathy Simkoff	Terry Taylor	John Jeter
Rick Cautela	Mark Hunter	Kim Stephens
Amir Windom	Maurice Slade	Randy Chase
John Latimer	Scott Morrill	Dave Sanchez
Scott Terry	Jason Popson	Steve Felton
Tom Schmitz	Rick Thomas	Jack Kilroy

Dave Felton	Marco Vukcevich	Kara Bresnahan
Jim Lamarco	Dan Peraino	David Klein
Dick Dale	Jeffrey Churchwell	Ari Nisman
Margie Alban	Sam Kirby	Eric Wilson
Amy Bennett	Wayne Forte	Tim Edwards
Eric Dimenstein	Matt Hickey	Frank Riley
Daniel Traci	Matt Pike	Tara Ruttle
Stormy Sheppard	Larry Webman	Marty Diamond
Steve Ferguson	Nadia Prescher	Brad Madison
Joy Collingbourne	Mitch Okmin	Cass Scripps
Brian Swanson	Marsh Vlasic	Neil Mandel
Scott Sokol	Barron Ruth	Trish Bauer
Tom Baggott	Howie Schnee	Jeff Epstein
Tim Sweetwood	Robbie Glick	Tracy Moody
Bradley Powell	Justin Simpson	Andrea Sweazy
Lindsay Lenehan	Ashley Grey	Alex Bain
Anthony Powers	Bryan Pauley	Jocelyn Hill
Kaitlin Rogers	Emma Popovich	Frank Soltysiak
Derek Sutcliffe	Kimber Weissert	Dave Vezdos
Jason Shelton	Larry Funderburk	Dave Davies
John Soeder	Munch Bishop	Quincy Taylor
Rob Bell	Joe Reid	Doan Buu
Trevor Moment	Rodney Rose	John Kalman
Chuck Yarborough	John Comprix	Kevin Mylott

Rob Runt

Brian Cook

Matt Vincik

Frank Longo

Sam Laponza

John Brown

Dave Siewert

Edsel Dope

Ken Jansen

Jeff Hatrix

Pat Lewis

Andrew Long

Kim Stephens

Amy Butterer

Shanna Hill

Mark Hunter

Justin Quade

Johnny Givens

Josh Schroeder

Shawn Vazinski

Michael Cardamone

Frato Laponza

Chuck Mills

Lisa Barr

CJ Pierce

Steve Dobo

Kevin Gilinski

Jim Petkewitz

Tom Hazart

Tom Loudermilk

Nikki Sechrist

Lydia Baynes

Scot Lee

Brett Russell

Steve Ganzhorn

Dan Habbyshaw

Jackie Laponza

Scott Beggs

Dave Adam

Paul Bassman

Dan Jansen

Tracy Moody

Waylon

Nick Mills

Jordan Goldstein

Kelly Richey

Pants Sechrist

Kenny Izizarry

Mike Salsbury

Also, special thanks to these artists & bands:

Slightly Stoopid

Mushroomhead

Creed

The Buzzcocks

Red Wanting Blue

MGK

Pepper

The Darkness

Tonic

Godsmack

Chip tha Ripper

Bizzy Bone

Switchfoot

Kid Cudi

The Wallflowers

Local H

iPhonic

Sponge

| Bellydance Superstars | Integrity | Kid Rock |
| Insane Clown Posse | The Fabulous Thunderbirds | The Presidents of the United States |

John and Dan would also like to thank all of the talented bands, musicians, artists, performers, and groups they have worked with over the years, including:

Mushroomhead	216	My Chemical Romance
Jay-Z	The Darkness	Snoop Dogg
The Game	Mindless Self Indulgence	Incubus
Kid Rock	Good Charlotte	O.A.R.
Mudvayne	George Clinton and the P. Funk	Converge
Fu Man Chu	Bellydance Superstars	Taking Back Sunday
Less Than Jake	I.C.P.	Breaking Benjamin
Three Days Grace	Creed	Godsmack
Gil Mantera's Party Dream	Chip tha Ripper	Kid Cudi
iPhonic	MGK	13 Faces
Disengage	Vanilla Ice	Unified Culture
State of Conviction	Dog Fashion Disco	Polkadot Cadaver
Gwar	Le Tigre	Stanley Clarke
Marcus Miller	Pieces of a Dream	Sizzla
Yngwie Malmsteen	LA Guns	Bret Michaels
Fozzy	Brides of Destruction	RATT
Beanie Man	Michael Schenker	The Hostile Omish
Man or Astroman?	System of a Down	Korn
Fear Factory	(hed) p.e.	Twiztid
Keeping Riley	Dangerous New Addiction	Empathic

A Greater Tomorrow	Spinn	Hope Leads
Scarecrow Hill	One Day's Notice	Cloud Nine Collapse
Anatoth	Tripod City	Wake Up
Jackie	Alien Ant Farm	Bongzilla
Cherry Poppin Daddies	Jimmie's Chicken Shack	Evil Beaver
Avail	The Queers	Great Big Sea
Carbon Leaf	Dropkick Murphy's	The Number Twelve Looks Like You
The Clarks	The Why Store	Red Wanting Blue
Genitorturers	Red Elvises	As I Lay Dying
Norma Jean	Dead Kennedy's	Misfits
The Addicts	Bone Thugs n Harmony	Sabotage
Garbage	Sepultura	Sloan
Fountains of Wayne	OK Go	Bad Boy Bill
Richard Humpty Vission	DJ Sneak	Soul Slinger
Scott Henry	Terrance Parker	7-Up
Aux 88	Cirrus	Rob Base and DJ EZ Rock
Reel Big Fish	Mike Jones	Paul Wall
Veruca Salt	Ice-T	Moe
Ekoostik Hookah	Zen Tricksters	North Mississippi Allstars
H2O	Powerman 5000	Overkill
Death Angel	Godhead	Secret Chiefs 3
Fantomas	Mr. Bungle	Brand New
Hello Goodbye	P.O.D.	Xzibit
Raekwon	Method Man	Ghostface Killah
Red Man	Andy Griggs	David Allan Coe

RZA	JGB	Hot Action Cop
Kitty	Gaelic Storm	Kings X
The Samples	The Cool Kids	The Living End
Liquid Soul	This Moment in Black History	Ringworm
Marcy's Playground	Product 86	"Stuttering" John
Artie Lang	As Tall As Lions	America Hi-Fi
Buckwheat Zydeco	CKY	Death By Stereo
Darkest Hour	El Vez	The Donnas
DJ Krush	Floetry	Everlast
Reliant K	Nashville Pussy	DJ Spooky
The Suicide Machines	JACKASS	Zebrahead
Edwin McCain	Nile	Soilwork
Sonata Arctica	Morbid Angel	Average White Band
Iced Earth	Kool Keith	KRS-One
John Mayall and the Bluesbreakers	r o u e	Keelhaul
Nevermore	Gov't Mule	Cobra Verde
RX Bandits	Life of Agony	Michael Franti and Spearhead
Candiria	DevilDriver	Cowboy Mouth
D.R.I.	Dredg	The Dillinger Escape Plan
Slash's Snakepit	Umphrey's McGee	Ice Cube
Slightly Stoopid	Pepper	Switchfoot
Sponge	Integrity	Godsmack
Local H	Danzig	B.O.B.
Hank Williams III	Bad Fish	DJ Maseo
Bleeding Through	Mad Ball	All That Remains
Puddle of Mud	Ming & FS	Q-Tip
Drowning Pool	?uestlove	Great White

Seven Mary Three	Swayze	Har Mar Superstar
John Cena	Toots And The Maytals	DJ Craze
Christopher Lawrence	Seb Fotaine	3 Inches of Blood
De La Soul	Exodus	In Flames
Kottonmouth Kings	Monster Magnet	Opeth
Thin Lizzy	Underoath	The Verve Pipe
Zox	Blackberry Smoke	Buckcherry
Virginia Coalition	Trivium	Meshuggah
Galactic	30 Seconds To Mars	Andrew W.K.
Kids in the Hall	Rusted Root	Lloyd Banks
Dieselboy	Ziggy Marley	Damian Marley
The Killers	Outkast	Snoop Dogg
Lamb of God	Motorhead	311
Hoobastank	Velvet Revolver	Nelly
Missy Elliot	D12	Guns N Roses
The Roots	Slipknot	NIN
The Black Keys	Midwest Reggae Fest	Hess Fest
Motion City Soundtrack	Voodoo Music Experience	

And finally, thanks to all of the amazing people that have helped us over the years with our music festivals and businesses:

Cleveland Music Festival	Houston Music Festival	Dallas Music Festival
Kansas City Music Festival	Seattle Music Festival	Detroit Music Festival
Buffalo Music Festival	Columbus Music Festival	Nashville Music Festival
The Barn	Sugarlight Productions	The Groove Shack
Reddstone	Duck Island	Heaven and Earth

& Peabody's

ABOUT THE AUTHORS
JOHN MICHALAK
John Michalak joined his first band at age 14 and began writing and recording music by age 15. By the time he was 19, John was in a semi successful group that played every club in Cleveland, Ohio. John's next band was called The AKT in which he played with Filter front man, Richard Patrick. John and Richard were best friends and band mates for over 2 years when Richard joined NIN, ultimately breaking up the band. Before The AKT broke up, they received heavy air play on every college radio station and sold out every show.

In 1995, John bought legendary concert venue, Peabody's Downunder. Two years later, John and his business partner developed a battle of the bands concert series that was so impressive that it helped shape the club and change the local scene in Cleveland at that time. John became locally know for selling out every local show he touched. Through the battle process, Peabody's was able to take relatively unknown bands and grow them into some of the biggest drawing bands in the city. It was during this time that John came up with the idea of a national production company that would specialize in helping local bands get shows and grow their followings.

In 2006, John and his brother, Dan Cull, started Gorilla Music. Within six years, Gorilla Music has become a household name to local musicians all across the country, producing local concerts and events in over 65 cities nationwide.

DAN CULL
Dan Cull is a music industry veteran and the most prolific talent buyer in the USA. At the age of 34, Dan has already produced over 8,000 events over the past 15 years. As a former owner of Cleveland's legendary Peabody's Concert Club and the current president of Gorilla Music (the nationally known concert production company) Dan has promoted acts such as Jay Z, My Chemical Romance, The Killers, Mudvayne, Lamb of God, Kid Cudi, Snoop Dogg, and The Darkness, just to name a few.

Dan is also the owner of an independent record label and works with bands both in and out of the studio. Dan also works closely with his Artist Development team to represent, manage, consult, and coach a number of emerging artists across the country.

Made in the USA
Middletown, DE
03 November 2022